T0127726

Many Millennials have no clear picture of what the Bible actually teaches about God, man, the past, and the future. In *Intimate and True*, Robert Ferris provides a readable summary of the Christian worldview. I highly recommend it.

Gary D. Chapman, Ph.D.
Author of *The Five Love Languages*

I am amazed at Robert Ferris's ability to simplify complex concepts and make them totally understandable. If you believe theology is either unintelligible or of no practical value, you need to read *Intimate and True*. Ferris makes theology both understandable and useful. The chapters are short and each explains issues we encounter on a daily basis. He is a gifted educator who takes complex truths and makes them comprehensible to the reader. I strongly recommend this book as it not only provides the foundational framework to study theology but also helps you love God.

Junias V. Venugopal, Ph.D.
Associate Dean of the School of Mission, Ministry, and Leadership
Wheaton College

In *Intimate and True*, Robert Ferris has written a pleasantly accessible introduction to Christian theology. The chapters are short, and the style is informal. Reading the book is like sitting down and having a series of conversations with the author. Dr. Ferris does not presume any prior theological training, and he avoids theological jargon. The theology in the book is solidly biblical and reflects both an extensive understanding of theological scholarship and years of thinking about the topics addressed.

John D. Harvey, Th.D.
Dean and Professor of New Testament
Columbia Biblical Seminary, Columbia International University

Robert Ferris has the gift of cutting through complex, excessively technical jargon and rendering deep insights into simple and memorable concepts. His work differs from conventional treatments of Bible doctrine, not in what it affirms, but in how it approaches almost every topic.

Ralph E. Enlow, Ed.D.
President, Association for Biblical Higher Education

*Intimate and True* is more than an overview of a Christian's foundational theological beliefs or doctrines. It is the loving voice of a grandfather answering questions of all who find themselves grappling with their beliefs and values. The reader is engaged with a mind that models thinking that flows from a biblical worldview, use of hermeneutical principles, and that thinks critically.

Milton Uecker, Ed.D.
Director, The Lowrie Center for Christian School Education
Professor of Education, Columbia International University

Robert Ferris is a theologian who aims to make sound biblical truth comprehensible to beginners and he has succeeded in this book. He presents solid theology in simple terms. I commend *Intimate and True* to all who want to understand better, and to communicate more effectively, the Bible's teaching concerning doctrine and Christian living.

Terrance L. Tiessen, Ph.D.
Professor of Systematic Theology and Ethics, Emeritus
Providence Theological Seminary, Otterburne, Manitoba

Professors, pastors, and teachers regularly face a great challenge—how to simplify complex subjects. This dilemma especially affects teachers of theology. Robert Ferris has done evangelicals a great service by writing this book. He has communicated the doctrinal truths of Scripture in a simple way. He has made deep spiritual truths both understandable and accessible. I recommend this book enthusiastically.

John Mark Terry, Ph.D.
Professor of Missions, Mid-America Baptist Seminary

In, *Intimate and True*, Robert Ferris has given the Church a treatment of Christianity's basic doctrines that is at once accessible, engaging, devotional, and biblically sound. Combining the best elements and methods of biblical and systematic theology, *Intimate and True* unfolds and organizes God's progressive revelation in a simple yet deeply profound and personal manner.

John R. Lillis. Ph.D.
Provost, Grace College and Seminary, Winona Lake, Indiana

Here is a theology book that clearly has been written for the benefit of all believers. Theologically serious yet incredibly accessible, robustly argued yet irenic and balanced, coherently organized and lucidly written, *Intimate and True* is an invaluable tool that every Christian interested in acquiring a firm understanding of the doctrines of Christian faith and their relevance for our time should have close at hand.

Dieumeme Noelliste, Ph.D.
Director, Vernon Grounds Institute of Public Ethics
Professor of Theological Ethics, Denver Seminary


*Intimate and True,* is a clearly-written and practical survey of basic Christian doctrine. With practical insight, this text shows where Christians should agree with one another and where they are free to hold different perspectives.

Larry Dixon, Ph.D.
Professor Emeritus, Columbia International University


There is a critical need for biblical literacy. Literacy, in turn, requires a theological framework that is true to Scripture. Robert Ferris has crafted an excellent tool to assist the church in addressing this need. He has a gift for clarity with strong biblical support. This is a fresh, relevant expression of a biblical theology that will ground a Christ follower for a lifelong walk.

Roy King, D.Min.
Church health leader, author, and consultant
Lead Pastor, Market Common Church, Myrtle Beach, SC


Robert Ferris has written an excellent theology that is accessible to millennials who want to know more about God's truth and that communicates truth into their generational values.

Jay McGuirk, Associate Pastor of Discipleship
Calvary Baptist Church, Winston-Salem, NC


This book not only is much needed, it is very well done.

Mark Young, Ph.D.
President, Denver Seminary

# Intimate & True

## BIBLE TRUTHS IN SIMPLE TERMS

ROBERT W. FERRIS

WESTBOW
PRESS®
A DIVISION OF THOMAS NELSON
& ZONDERVAN

Unless otherwise indicated, scripture is taken from The Holy Bible, English
Standard Version® (ESV®) Copyright © 2001 by Crossway, a publishing
ministry of Good News Publishers. All rights reserved. ESV Text Edition: 2016

Scripture taken from the King James Version of the Bible.

Scripture quotations marked (NLT) are taken from the Holy Bible,
New Living Translation, copyright ©1996, 2004, 2015 by Tyndale
House Foundation. Used by permission of Tyndale House Publishers,
Inc., Carol Stream, Illinois 60188. All rights reserved.

Scripture quotations marked (NIV) are taken from the Holy Bible, New
International Version®, NIV®. Copyright © 1973, 1978, 1984, 2011 by Biblica,
Inc.™ Used by permission of Zondervan. All rights reserved worldwide. www.
zondervan.com The "NIV" and "New International Version" are trademarks
registered in the United States Patent and Trademark Office by Biblica, Inc.™

WestBow Press books may be ordered through booksellers or by contacting:

WestBow Press
A Division of Thomas Nelson & Zondervan
1663 Liberty Drive
Bloomington, IN 47403
www.westbowpress.com
1 (866) 928-1240

Because of the dynamic nature of the Internet, any web addresses or
links contained in this book may have changed since publication and
may no longer be valid. The views expressed in this work are solely those
of the author and do not necessarily reflect the views of the publisher,
and the publisher hereby disclaims any responsibility for them.

Any people depicted in stock imagery provided by Getty Images are
models, and such images are being used for illustrative purposes only.
Certain stock imagery © Getty Images.

ISBN: 978-1-9736-3416-4 (sc)
ISBN: 978-1-9736-3418-8 (hc)
ISBN: 978-1-9736-3417-1 (e)

Library of Congress Control Number: 2018908286

Print information available on the last page.

WestBow Press rev. date: 11/13/2018

THIS BOOK IS FOR

--------------------------------

Anna
Daniel and Will
Rayah and Kaelyn

--------------------------------

And for all others
of their generation
who desire to
understand and obey
God's Holy Scriptures.

# CONTENTS

# A NOTE FROM THE AUTHOR

Thank you for picking up this book. I hope you will find it helpful in understanding and expressing your faith.

The beginnings of this book stretch back forty-five years. In 1973, I was assigned to teach a one-year course in theology at Febias College of Bible, in the Philippines. I titled that course "Bible Truths" because that is what I intended to be the focus of the course. As I taught, I also learned. I learned that the task of the theologian is not simply to perpetuate answers from past questions but to show that the Bible contains answers to questions of people today. I also learned that the questions on the minds of my Filipino students were different from those of American students or of 17th and 18th Century European students.

In the process of preparing for and teaching that and other courses at Febias, helped by my students and many teachers and scholars before me, I worked out my understanding of God's truth. Since then, I also have taught theology at Asian Theological Seminary and at Columbia Biblical Seminary and School of Missions, now part of Columbia International University. Along the way, I discovered that my job was bigger than I had anticipated and that God's Word is richer than I had realized.

Forty years later, I had the privilege of teaching a Bible doctrines course for Anna, my home-schooled granddaughter. At the end of our course, Anna assigned me to write this book. Writing it has given me an opportunity to look, again, at the things God has taught me from his Word and to marvel at the beauty and consistency of his truth.

Each chapter in this book concludes with a section titled, "Let's Talk About It." The questions posed typically do not have right or wrong answers. Rather than asking you to repeat something included in the chapter, they invite you to extend your thinking about the topic—to examine the relationship of these topics to those of previous chapters or to explore implications of the things you've read for your own life and relationships.

You will find the chapters of this book most beneficial if you discuss them with others. Ideally, your conversation partner or partners also will have read the chapters you discuss. If you don't have a dialogue partner, even internal dialogue is beneficial as you examine and explore these truths in your own mind. This will require you to pause and reflect, rather than moving immediately to the next chapter. In reflection, in making the truth of Scripture our own, its enlightening and transforming power is released into our lives.

Since this book is titled *Intimate and True*, you won't be surprised to find that intimacy is a major theme running throughout the book. That's appropriate, since intimacy is what God seeks in his relationship with us. Truth—specifically, the truth of God's Word, the Bible—also is affirmed over and over. You will find many, many references to the Bible. Some scholars speak poorly of "proof texting," as though citing Scripture somehow is inappropriate. Of course, Scripture may be twisted to say things that were not intended and Satan is a master of such distortions. It is my conviction and experience, however, that the meaning of God's word usually is clear when read in context. When I cite Bible verses in describing God's truth, I expect you to read those verses in context to assure that they mean what they appear to say. If a verse, contextually interpreted, expresses the truth it appears to state, then I see no problem in citing it when discussing God's truth.

That raises an important point. When I taught theology at Febias College of Bible, I told my students they never should believe me; they should test everything I tell them. If the concepts I teach are supported by the Bible, then I want students to believe those truths because they rest on the authority of God's inspired word, not because of any authority they may attribute to me. If, on the other hand, the concepts I teach are not supported by the Bible, then my students certainly should not believe them! I expect you to do the same as you read.

Robert W. Ferris
May 21, 2018

# CHAPTER 1

## A Place to Begin

A discussion of God's revealed truth could begin almost anywhere since God's revealed truth is consistent throughout. It is common for a discussion of Christian theology to begin with the doctrine of God, his existence, his attributes, and his work.[1] It also would be reasonable to begin with human beings, what makes us unique, why life is so difficult, God's provision for us now, and his plan for our future. Or one could begin with Jesus Christ, with the church, or even with heaven—the end point of biblical revelation.

It seems reasonable to me, however, to begin where the Bible does, with the origin of the universe (Genesis 1:1). Why is there something rather than nothing? Why do you and I, this physical world, and the stellar universe exist rather than an infinite void? Many people tend to ignore the question of origins, or to assume that this universe always has existed.

If you stop to think about it, assuming that the universe always has existed doesn't square with everything we know about matter. All our experience supports the principle of entropy—that undisturbed matter progresses toward decay, rather than progressing toward higher levels of organization or existence in a steady state. Furthermore, the principle of cause and effect is well established; no evidence supports the suggestion that, without a cause, something spontaneously appeared from nothing. It never happens! Yet, this world exists.

The (totally unsupported) suggestion that an infinite number of other universes preceded this one offers no relief, since it simply

---

[1] We use male pronouns when referring to God because the Bible does but we understand that gender does not apply to God.

pushes the problem of origins back to an earlier point. Thus, something must be eternal, but we have no reason to think it is matter.

In fact, the Bible tells us, something is eternal. Furthermore, according to the Bible, the eternal also is personal and this eternal, personal being is God. This is good news, since it assures us that personality is not a celestial afterthought or the product of a fortuitous electro-chemical interaction. Personality lies at the very heart of the universe!

Healthy personality requires social relationships—to communicate with and love other persons. Although we do not understand this (because it is a form of existence which lies outside our experience), God has told us that he exists in three persons, each of whom independently knows and thinks and feels and wills and communicates and loves, and yet all of whom share exactly the same qualities and capacities—and exist as one being. Thus, not only does personality lie at the very heart of the universe but so does relationship and social interaction.

But wait! There is more good news: This personal God who always existed in perfect completeness, at some point in the remote past decided that he wanted to expand the circle of his relationships to include other beings who would love him freely. He did not take this decision because he needed to, only because he wanted to. Thus, the Christian message really is a love story.

In order to provide an appropriate venue for this love story to play out, God created the universe, not from pre-existing matter (there was none!), but "out of nothing." God then created human beings "like himself"—with personality, intelligence, emotion, and will. He created them male and female so they could learn mutual submission and could experience loving another person whom they can see as preparation for loving himself, whom they cannot see. He gave them families so they could understand a creator's love for his children and the heartbreak of watching children walk away.

Sadly, that's what the first humans did and that's what we all do. Rather than submitting to the God of the universe, we assert our own independence and rebel against his authority. This state of rebellion has fundamentally changed us—our bodies, our intelligence, our emotions, and our will. It also changes our relationships to other persons; it marks our societies in twisted and destructive ways. As a result and as a reflection of our rebellion, God also has given us a decaying and dangerous world.

Our rebellion is not the worst of it; there is nothing we can do to fix our broken relationship. We not only have offended God's person, we have violated his character—the very foundation of his eternal existence. Ignoring our offense or pretending it does not exist is not an option.

The best news of all is this: The eternal, all-powerful, holy, and just God who created the universe and who created us for fellowship with himself recognized the hopelessness of our situation and personally chose to do what only he could do. He took the punishment which we deserve. In this way he satisfied the demands of justice for our rebellion, and reopened access to fellowship with himself. The only other thing required is that we acknowledge and abandon our lifestyle of rebellion and accept the gift of restoration which God offers to us. In the Bible, Paul says that God took the penalty of our sin "to show himself both just and the justifier of those who put their faith in him" (Romans 3:26).

How did he do this? He did it by first becoming one of us. The divine second person of the Triune God voluntarily accepted the limitations of human existence; he entered the world he had created through a human birth canal and lived as a Jewish boy in 1st Century Galilee. This man, known as Jesus of Nazareth, faced life as we do except he never embraced the rebellion which estranges us from himself. He lived a perfect life and died a perfect death in order to pay the penalty for human rebellion and open access to restored fellowship between the eternal God of the universe and human beings whom he loves so deeply. Furthermore, God, in the person of this same Jesus, returned to life three days after he had been declared dead in order to demonstrate that everything required for reconciliation between ourselves and our creator already has been done. That's how much he loves us.

Sadly, however, that's not the end of this love story. The reconciliation which God achieved by taking our rebellion into himself is ineffective until we, individually, as families, and as communities, abandon our rebellious ways and accept this gift of loving restoration. Even with all God has done for us, we still can frustrate his eternal quest for loving companionship with ourselves.

In fact, many people do. Having rejected God's love, they effectively opt to bear the consequences of their rebellion—total alienation from God and eternal disintegration of the personal and social core of their being.

Thankfully, there are others—the Bible refers to them as a vast crowd, too large to count (Revelation 7:9)—who have accepted God's offer of reconciliation and have abandoned their rebellious lifestyle. These acknowledge the ultimate reality—that God exists and that he fully deserves our humble obedience and heartfelt service.

The difference between those who have been reconciled to God and those who continue to reject his provision of reconciliation is so great that the Bible refers to them as a new race (Romans 5:14-17; 1 Corinthians 15:45-49). Although opportunity still is open for others to acknowledge our rebellion and to accept God's gift, he has told us that will not always be the case. The time is coming when God's patience with rebellious people finally will reach an end. At that time he will release this creation from its present flawed state, recreating a perfect world, and will realize the free and open relationship of love with his people which he initially envisioned. At that time, also, those who stubbornly have chosen to persist in rebellion against him will experience the full consequence of their choice. This is a dreadful prospect.

Does it surprise you that the reason for our existence lies in God's desire for relationship with us? For a long time, Biblical Christians[2] have focused on status; the question often asked is, "Have you been saved?" (Note the past tense.) The Christian message is not about getting our ticket punched for heaven. God is not a divine conductor, checking to see who is going to heaven. God is a divine lover; he desires relationship—personal, intimate relationship—with us now and even more fully in the future, in a new and sin-free environment. The Bible tells us that then "we shall be like him, because we shall see him as he is" (1 John 3:2). That doesn't mean we shall become gods—there is and ever will be only one God—but we shall be like him in character (pure, just, holy), freed from every impediment to intimate relationship with the God of the universe.

Intimacy need not be postponed for the future, however. Through study of and obedience to the truth revealed in the Bible and through attention to the promptings of the Holy Spirit, we can grow

---

[2] For an explanation of my use of the term "Biblical Christians," see Appendix A.

in intimacy with God now. That is what he desires. It is what we also desire at the core of our being. As we refocus on developing intimacy, rather than on certifying status, God's purpose is realized and our personhood finds its ultimate fulfillment.

As servants of God—having adopted his perspective on this world—we have a profound responsibility to act as his agents to invite others to embrace the reconciliation we enjoy and to heal the brokenness of our societies.

This is the intimacy and truth we will explore together.

**Let's Talk About It**

• What significance do you see in the suggestion that the ultimate and only eternal reality in the universe is not matter but a person?

• How does it make you feel to realize that God desires an intimate, personal relationship with you, that this is the reason he created you?

# CHAPTER 2

## What Is Truth?

The nature of truth is a big issue today. The reigning epistemology (i.e., the theory of truth) in universities, the major media, and popular culture is constructivism. Constructivism begins from the observation that we all start from our own experience. As we attempt to make sense of our experience (with the help of our culture and our social networks, including our families) we "construct" opinions about what is real, what is good, and how things and events are related. We weave these into a perspective that we use to interpret life experiences and that we assume to be truth.

Constructivism naturally leads toward relativism. Because each of us constructs our own view of truth and because, for all of us, our experience is limited, no one can say definitively that his or her view of truth is absolutely correct. Thus, it is expected today that we will be tolerant of one another. ("Tolerant," used in this way, means that we acknowledge the validity of the other person's "truth.") As the 19th Century German philosopher, Friedrich Nietzsche said, "There are many eyes.... Consequently, there are many truths, hence there is no Truth."[3]

This combination of constructivism and radical relativism is known as "postmodernism." It is "post-modern" because it has left behind the assumptions of philosophical "modernism." Modernism is a philosophy developed in the late 17th and 18th Centuries that became the engine of the scientific revolution, industrialization, democratic political theory, and much of the culture we enjoy today. Modernism assumed the reality and order of the natural world and the existence of absolute truth. According to modernism, truth

---

[3] Friedrich Nietzsche, *The Will to Power*, Section 540.

claims can be tested against reality and thus validated or falsified (i.e., disproven). Truth claims that cannot be subjected to empirical testing, therefore, may be dismissed as mere opinion, tradition, or superstition.

Modernity (another name for philosophical modernism) presented Biblical Christians with a dilemma. While Biblical Christians rejected the suggestion that all religion is mere superstition (since it cannot be scientifically demonstrated), they knew that truth is absolute. Jesus Christ is not just "a truth," he is "the truth." Postmodernity is even more hostile toward Biblical Christianity, however, since it asserts all truth claims are relative. As a result, Biblical Christians have tended to denounce postmodernity as false.

Actually, there are aspects of truth in postmodern epistemology. Our concept of truth is constructed; each person develops her or his own understanding of truth from experience, including experience mediated by family and culture. We don't arrive with a data chip implant that enables us to view the world and conceive truth objectively. That our understanding of truth is constructed does not mean, however, that it is impossible to assess the validity of my conception of what is true versus yours. Truth claims can be tested. Everyone must live in the world which God created. If our understanding of truth does not match the reality of God's world, life can become very difficult. If you believe you can walk through a wall, you are likely to get bruised. (That's why there are many more postmodern professors in the humanities and social science departments of major universities than in the hard sciences that research the physical world.)

In many areas of life, it also is true that truth is relative. Cultural norms vary from one culture to another; whether we eat with chop sticks, with a fork and knife, with only a spoon, or with our fingers is not a matter of right and wrong, those are just differences. Personal tastes vary from individual to individual; no one considers it a problem that my wife prefers chocolate ice cream and I like vanilla. That some things obviously are relative, however, does not imply that everything is relative. We don't have to abandon the existence of absolutes.

We still need to be able to decide what to believe, to distinguish between what is true and what is false. God anticipated this when dealing with the people of Israel. In their context, the question was how to recognize a true prophet, a prophet who could be trusted to speak God's message faithfully. God provides two, complementary answers to that question in the book of Deuteronomy.

In Deuteronomy 13, Moses instructs Israel on discerning true and false prophets:

> If a prophet or a dreamer of dreams arises among you and gives you a sign or a wonder, and the sign or wonder that he tells you comes to pass, and if he says, 'Let us go after other gods,' which you have not known, 'and let us serve them,' you shall not listen to the words of that prophet or that dreamer of dreams. For the Lord your God is testing you, to know whether you love the Lord your God with all your heart and with all your soul. You shall walk after the Lord your God and fear him and keep his commandments and obey his voice, and you shall serve him and hold fast to him. But that prophet or that dreamer of dreams shall be put to death, because he has taught rebellion against the Lord your God, who brought you out of the land of Egypt and redeemed you out of the house of slavery, to make you leave the way in which the Lord your God commanded you to walk. So you shall purge the evil from your midst. (Deuteronomy 13:1-5)

In this passage, God provides the first test of a prophet. Notice that the prophet arrives claiming to represent God. He announces a miracle to prove his authenticity and the miracle occurs. Then the prophet announces a message—"Let us go after other gods"— which is rationally inconsistent with prior revelation. God says, "Stone him; he is not a true prophet." The first test, therefore, is a rational test. If any truth claim is rationally inconsistent with God's previously revealed truth, it must be rejected. It is false.

Later, Moses assures Israel that God will provide new leadership for the nation following his death. This naturally raises the question as to how this new leader—also a prophet, like Moses—will be recognized.

> I will raise up for them a prophet like you from among their brothers. And I will put my words in his mouth, and he shall speak to them all that I command him. And whoever will not listen to my words that he shall speak in my name, I myself will require it of him. But the prophet who presumes to speak a word in my name that I have not

commanded him to speak, or who speaks in the name of other gods, that same prophet shall die.' And if you say in your heart, 'How may we know the word that the Lord has not spoken?'—when a prophet speaks in the name of the Lord, if the word does not come to pass or come true, that is a word that the Lord has not spoken; the prophet has spoken it presumptuously. You need not be afraid of him. (Deuteronomy 18:18-22)

In this case, the prophet arrives and announces a miracle but the miracle does not happen. God says, "Stone him; you don't need to be afraid of him." The second test, therefore, is an empirical test. If any truth claim is inconsistent with the empirical realities of this physical world, it must be rejected. It is false.

When we look at these two tests, we see that they both are tests of consistency. Truth is consistent. That's why consistency—rational and empirical—is an appropriate test of truth. When God says that he is truth, therefore, it is appropriate for us to understand that he is completely and eternally consistent.

How can we tell, then, what is absolute? Where do we draw the line between relative and absolute? We know that God's truth is absolute. In the Bible he has revealed truth about himself and truth about ourselves that transcends cultural and personal boundaries. So in the areas of theology and ethics, we have absolute standards.[4] God's creation also presents absolute realities that test human truth claims. Beyond the revealed and the empirical, however, Christians can embrace and celebrate relativism in many areas of human experience.

In the 20th and 21st Centuries, Christians often have found themselves defending their faith against scientific truth claims that appear to conflict with the Bible. The diagram below affords a helpful perspective on these apparent conflicts.

---

[4] Nevertheless, the application of those standards may vary depending on context and culture—e.g., modesty is a trans-cultural, biblical standard but what constitutes modesty varies from one culture to another.

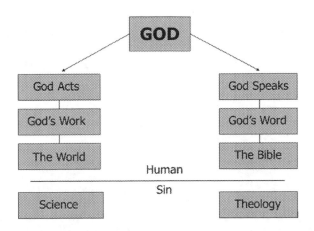

If we begin with the understanding that God is perfectly consistent, then we will recognize that God's acts and his speech are consistent. Therefore, his work and his word are consistent, and the world (the result of God's creative work) and the Bible (the result of God's revelatory speech) are consistent. We don't always see that consistency, however; sometimes our science (i.e., our best interpretation of the world God has created) and our theology (i.e., our best interpretation of the truth that God has revealed in the Bible) are inconsistent. Sometimes this simply is because the data we have are partial. We need more data to see the whole picture, to recognize the consistency of God's truth. At other times, it's because we view both the world and the Bible through sin-distorted lenses. Often we don't want to know the truth because it convicts us or because it challenges our aspirations to autonomy. So we bend the truth—rarely knowingly, but often subconsciously—to make it better fit our warped desires and, in the process, it becomes inconsistent with the truth God has revealed (cf. Romans 1:21-23).

When the truth claims of science and theology conflict, we can be sure one of three things is true: Either our science is correct and our theology is wrong (Remember Galileo?), or our theology is correct and our science is wrong (Think of the creative ways naturalistic scientists have tried to explain the origin of the universe.), or both our science and our theology are wrong. If the truth claims of our science and our theology conflict, however, both cannot be right. If both were right, they would agree because truth is grounded in God and God is consistent.

The question of truth is important because it shapes everything we do. It's important to recognize, therefore, that although we construct our own understanding of what is real, what is good, and how things work, our understanding and everyone else's can be tested against the realities of this world that God created and against God's revelation in Scripture. If any truth claim is consistent in both regards—i.e., both empirically and rationally—it can be trusted. If not, it must be rejected or, at least, held in doubt until more data are available.

**Let's Talk About It**

- Name two or three topics on which our culture, today, expects us to acknowledge that there may be more than one right answer, more than one "right way" to act.

- How do these topics stand the two tests of truth identified in in this chapter? If any fails one or both tests, which did it fail? What evidence exposes it is false, even though it claims to be true?

# CHAPTER 3

## The God Who Is

When Moses asked God to tell him his name, God said, "My name is 'The God who is.'" (That is the meaning of the expression, "I am," in Exodus 3:14.) Existence is God's distinguishing quality. Everything else has had a beginning and most other things will come to an end. This universe is not eternal. Human life is not eternal. Even the angels and demons are not eternal but God is eternal; he just is. He always has existed. He always will exist. He is "the God who is."

When the Bible says that God is eternal (Deuteronomy 33:27; Romans 16:26), it means he always has and always will exist. St. Augustine, in the 4th Century, struggled with this concept. Augustine studied and taught Platonic philosophy before he became a Christian. Plato reasoned that change is an inherent aspect of time. Anything that exists in time changes. Therefore, he reasoned, the final cause of all that is—what he termed "The Unmoved Mover"—must exist outside of time. Augustine identified the God of the Bible with Plato's "Unmoved Mover" and concluded that the Biblical God must exist in an "Eternal Now," outside of time. Nothing in Scripture supports this idea but Augustine's suggestion is widely accepted and taught today.

There are several reasons (in addition to lack of biblical support) for rejecting this idea. Time is not an object that could be created, as often is suggested.[5] Time is a relationship, like distance. Meters and miles do not exist and neither do minutes and years. Meters, miles, minutes, and years only are units we use to describe spatial

---

[5] The King James Version translates Revelation 10:6, "...that there should be time no longer." The apparent meaning of this verse was popularized in the hymn, "When the roll is called up yonder and time shall be no more...." This is an unfortunate translation, however, at least by modern usage. More recent scholars accurately translate the text "...that there would be no more delay."

or temporal proximity. For us, events happen in sequence, in a before-and-after order. Just as you are reading the words on this page one at a time, so we meet the events of our lives one at a time, one after another. Also, events have duration—they continue for different lengths of time. Some things last only an instant but others continue for years or centuries. When we look to the Scriptures, we find that sequence and duration are aspects of God's experience as well (Psalm 90:1-2; John 17:5, 24; Revelation 16:5). He is "the God who is," the one who always has existed and who always will exist (Psalm 145:13; Isaiah 44:6; Revelation 1:8). He experiences time as we do except he has existed from the infinite past and he will exist into the infinite future.

Eternity—time infinitely extended into the past and future—is a difficult concept to grasp. Perhaps the best description comes from John Newton's hymn, "Amazing Grace."

> When we've been there ten thousand years
> > Bright shining as the sun,
> We've no less days to sing God's praise
> > Than when we'd first begun.

Newton understood the concept of infinite time. That's what the Bible means when it teaches that "God is eternal."

Not only is God infinite in time, he is infinite in other ways, as well. He is infinite in power. Theologians refer to this as God's "omnipotence." Because God is infinite in power, he can do whatever he wants. God never is limited in his ability to do what he wants because he lacks the needed capacity.

Science tells us that the universe is expanding and, by reasoning backward, we conclude that everything that now exists began with a "Big Bang." So, what existed to go "bang"? If anything physical existed, then matter is eternal and we know that cannot be. Everything we know about matter belies that conclusion. There was a "bang," however. Genesis tells us that God said, "Let there be light and [BANG!] there was light" (Genesis 1:3). God created the universe and everything in it out of nothing. He can do that. Indeed, he can do whatever he wants. He never desires to do something but realizes that he lacks the needed power. He is "omnipotent."

God also is infinite in his presence. As the psalmist, David, wrote,

Where shall I go from your Spirit?
Or where shall I flee from your presence?
If I ascend to heaven, you are there!
If I make my bed in Sheol, you are there!
(Psalm 139:7-8)

We cannot run from God, there is no place to hide, God always is present. Theologians refer to this as God's "omnipresence," but what does it mean? How can God be in North Carolina and in New York and in Illinois and in the Philippines and in Ecuador and in South Africa and in Russia, and in... (You get the picture.) all at the same time? If God could be diffused, like the atmosphere we breathe, that could be. God is not a formless substance, however; God is a person. We'll see more specifically what that means in the next chapter but a person has location. A person cannot be in multiple places at once.

Whenever the Bible teaches something that seems illogical or irrational, we can be sure that the problem exists in our thinking since (as we already have seen) God is totally consistent. The problem with our understanding of God's omnipresence, it turns out, is that we begin from ourselves; we assume that God must exist in our presence. Everything in the room in which I sit currently is in my presence but everything outside this room is not present to me. We naturally assume that the doctrine of "omnipresence" means that God exists in this room, in my presence, and in the presence of every other person on earth and heaven.

Suppose, however, that we flip it around; suppose, instead of beginning with me, we begin with God. Now, we understand "omnipresence" to mean that everything that exists is in God's presence. There's nothing illogical about that! In fact, that's just what David said as he was inspired by the Holy Spirit to write Psalm 139.

That God is omnipresent truly is awesome, as well as very sobering. Every moment you and I live in God's presence. He always knows us intimately. This also is comforting; because I exist in his presence, God never is unaware of my situation or so remote that he cannot help when I am in need.

God also is infinite in his knowledge; he knows everything. He knows everything in the past, everything now present, and everything that will happen in the future. He knows things that are determined (e.g., the orbit of the moon and the planets, so we can create tide charts, predict solar eclipses, and be confident of the location of Mars when a rocket gets there) and he knows things that he allows us freely to decide (e.g., what we'll have for breakfast tomorrow morning and what we'll be doing five years from now). He also knows everything that could happen (i.e., possibilities) and everything that does happen (i.e., actualities). Theologians refer to this as God's "omniscience."

It is not hard for us to understand how God can know past, determined and free, actualities. We call that "history" and although no one has a comprehensive knowledge of everything that has happened, it's not hard for us to understand how God could know all that. It's also not hard for us to understand how God can know present actualities, since we experience life daily, as well. Nor is it difficult to understand God's knowledge of future, determined, actualities; we also know that. (Think about tide charts.)

What we cannot understand is God's knowledge of future, free, actualities—the things that people freely will choose in the future. Yet the Bible tells us that God knew how Pharaoh would respond to Moses' request before Moses had communicated God's command. Note that God did not say to Moses, "Now, my best guess is that Pharaoh will refuse to let the people go." Absolutely not! He said, "I know that the king of Egypt will not let you go unless compelled by a mighty hand" (Exodus 3:19).

How did God know how Pharaoh would respond? Did he cause Pharaoh to respond as he did? If that were the case, then Pharaoh is not responsible for his action and it would not be fair to punish him for the choice made. God does punish Pharaoh, however. Furthermore, if God causes the choices we make, then freedom only is an illusion and our love for God or rejection of him also is determined by God. That can't be! God clearly holds us responsible for the choices we make, including our choice whether or not to acknowledge him as God (cf. Matthew 23:37; 25:31-46).

Another possible explanation may be that God is the ultimate mathematician. Perfectly knowing the past and present, he calculates all factors and predicts the future with absolute accuracy. That also can't be. We can predict determined events but free events cannot be predicted in this way. Humans are not robots, programmed to respond in totally predictable ways.

The best way to understand God's knowledge of future, free, actualities is to recognize that our knowledge—unlike his— is limited. Our understanding, furthermore, is limited by our experience. People who live in tropical jungles cannot comprehend "snow." Snow is not irrational, it simply is outside the realm of their experience. Likewise, knowledge of future, free, actualities is beyond our experience. That does not make it illogical or irrational; we just cannot understand what is beyond our experience. The Bible clearly teaches, however, that it is not beyond God's experience. He knows everything. That includes everything past, present, and future, all possibilities and actualities, and all determined and free events. Everything!

These four qualities—God's eternality, omnipotence, omnipresence, and omniscience—sometimes are referred to as God's "essential attributes." That is, they describe God's "essence," how he exists.

In addition, God has revealed various aspects of his character. These may be termed God's moral attributes. God is:

- Holy (Leviticus 19:2; Revelation 4:8)[6]
- Just (Ezekiel 18:25-29; Romans 2:11)[7]
- Loving; he naturally expresses persistent love (Lamentations 3:22-23; 1 John 4:7-11)[8]

Throughout the Scriptures we see these moral attributes demonstrated in the ways God relates to people. Furthermore, his character is unchanging (Malachi 3:6; James 1:17).[9] We always can be confident he is holy and just and loving. That is the kind of God he is.

Such a great God deserves our worship and such a morally perfect God deserves our emulation. In fact, Jesus said, "you must be perfect as your heavenly Father is perfect" (Matthew 5:48). There are issues that complicate that which we will explore later. For now, we should recognize that God expects us to strive to develop our character to be like his.

---

[6] See also Isaiah 57:15; Habakkuk 1:13; 1 John 1:5.
[7] See also 2 Chronicles 19:7; Nehemiah 9:33; 2 Peter 2:9.
[8] See also Deuteronomy 7:7-8; Psalm 5:12; 89:30-33; Jeremiah 31:3.
[9] See also Numbers 23:19; Psalm 119:89-90; Hebrews 13:8.

**Let's Talk About It**

- Of the four "essential" attributes discussed—God's eternality, omnipotence, omnipresence, and omniscience—which do you find most difficult to understand? Can you identify why?

- Are the four "moral" attributes mentioned—God's holiness, justice, love, and changelessness—any less "essential" to whom God is than the others? Why? Which do you find most comforting? Why?

# CHAPTER 4

## Our Personal, But Unique, God

This God who exists is both very much like us and very, very different from us. He is like us (or, more accurately, we are like him) in that he is personal. He is very, very different in that he exists as a Trinity. Both of these concepts deserve exploration.

It is not an accident that humans are persons who can think, who experience joy and sorrow, who make choices, who are self-aware, and who communicate and covenant and love. The God who exists possesses all these abilities, as well. He is a person (actually, he is three persons but we will come to that in a bit) and he created us as personal beings, like himself, so he could relate to us person-to-person. As a result, we can learn a lot about him by looking at ourselves.

Like us, God is real. We can imagine things that do not exist but we do not have difficulty distinguishing the real from the unreal. Just as you and I are real, God is real. In fact, Isaiah and Jeremiah both argued the most important difference between the God of the Bible and idols worshipped by Israel's neighbors is that God is real and the "gods" represented by idols are not (Isaiah 45:18-23; Jeremiah 10:1-16).

One sure test of reality is whether a person or thing can affect that which is known to be real. Indeed, this is exactly the test Darius applied as he approached the lion's den where Daniel had spent the night. Darius and everyone present knew the lions were real; they could hear them roaring! Only a real God could rescue Daniel from those lions. So, after a sleepless night, Darius called to Daniel and asked, "Has your God...been able to deliver you from the lions?" (Daniel 6:20). When Daniel assured Darius that he was safe, Darius drew the obvious conclusion that God is real because was able to protect Daniel from real lions (Daniel 6:25-28).

Daniel's experience is not an isolated event; the Bible is full of accounts in which God changed physical realities in order to achieve his purposes and to protect his people. The deliverance of God's people from Egypt by parting the Red Sea (Exodus 14:21-22) is just one example. The miracles of Jesus and of the prophets and apostles lead to the same conclusion. God is very real!

Like us, God also possesses intellect; he can know and think and plan. In the previous chapter we saw that God is "omniscient"— that he knows everything. That does not mean, however, that God is a huge databank, filled with static information. Rather, the Bible describes God as observing (Genesis 16:13; Job 28:23-24), remembering (Psalm 105:8; 2 Corinthians 7:15), and planning (Psalm 33:11; Jeremiah 29:11). This does not surprise us because we do these things, too. This is another way we understand that God is personal.

Like us, God also experiences emotion. The Bible tells us, at different times, he is happy (Deuteronomy 30:9; Jeremiah 9:24), sad, disappointed, or grieved (Genesis 6:5-6; Isaiah 63:10), or angry (Amos 5:21; Hebrews 10:29). His emotions are not as mercurial as ours nor do his emotions blur his thinking or trigger blind reactions as ours sometimes do. Nevertheless, God's emotions are as real as ours.

Like us, God also possesses a will; he can make choices. Aren't you thankful that God chose to create this world and to create people (Genesis 1:1, 26)! Even before that, however, the Bible tells us that God anticipated our rebellion and chose to provide restoration of relationship through the life and death of Jesus (Ephesians 1:4). Indeed, among all the generations of humans who have lived on this earth, even before creation God chose us who have identified with Christ to be his very own people (1 Peter 1:2; 2:9). Throughout history, God has continued to make choices. He chose Abram to become the ancestor of Jesus (Genesis 12:1-3; 18:19), he chose David to be king over Israel (1 Samuel 16:10-12), and he chose the nation of Israel to be his servant and a light to the nations (Isaiah 41:9-10; 49:5-7). God continues to choose to love us, to bless us, and to invite all people into relationship with himself, but the day is coming when he will choose to hold people accountable for the choices they have made. With that in mind, the writer of Hebrews reminds us, "It is a fearful thing to fall into the hands of the living God" (Hebrews 10:28-31).

Like us, God is self-aware. Just as we are aware of our own identity, can observe our own thought processes, and can weigh pros and cons as we dialogue with ourselves, so God shares this same self-awareness. Over and over, God reminded Israel though the prophets that he alone is God (Exodus 8:10; Isaiah 45:5-6). God also is aware of his own thoughts (Isaiah 55:8-9), intentions (Jeremiah 23:20; 30:24), and plans (Jeremiah 29:11). Paul specifically draws an analogy between our self-awareness and God's self-awareness when writing to the Corinthians. He said that just as only I know what I am thinking, so only God knows his own thoughts (1 Corinthians 2:11).

Finally, like us, God experiences personal relationships, within the Trinity and with the other persons he has created; he communicates, covenants, and loves. Communication is a distinctive characteristic of personhood. While animals may communicate at a basic level, among persons, communication is a highly developed gift. We share our thoughts and emotions, our concerns and desires with other persons. From the first chapter of the Bible, when God said, "Let there be light," to the last chapter of the Bible, in which Jesus said, "Surely I am coming soon," God speaks. Indeed, the sixty-six books of the Bible are God's "Word," his inspired message to the human race (2 Timothy 3:16-17). Furthermore, God the Holy Spirit continues to speak to people today—sometimes quietly and internally (Romans 8:16) but also sometimes very dramatically through dreams and visions. Jesus said that the Holy Spirit will convict the world (i.e., those aligned against him) of sin, righteousness, and judgment (John 16:8-11) and will comfort and guide his disciples (John 16:12-15).

A second capacity unique to persons is to make commitments. We may refer to them as promises, pledges, vows, or covenants, but the common theme is commitment to do or provide something in the future. Only persons make such commitments and a person's esteem by others is closely tied to his or her faithfulness in doing what has been promised. The Bible records God's promises to Abraham (Genesis 12:1-3; 15:4-6), Moses (Exodus 3:15-17), Joshua (Joshua 1:1-5), David (2 Samuel 7:8-16), and to the nation of Israel through many of the prophets (cf. Isaiah 44:24-28; Jeremiah 31:31-34; Ezekiel 39:25-29). Jesus also promised to send the Holy Spirit (John 14:15-16) and to come again to be reunited with his people (John 14:2-3).

The self-sacrificial commitment we know as love also is a mark of personhood. John tells us that "God is love" (1 John 4:8)—it is his nature to give of himself for the humans he created. This he did on the cross (1 John 4:9-10; Romans 5:6-8). Love among persons has an emotional dimension (for which we are thankful!) but ultimately, love entails placing the good of the other above one's own. This we see supremely in Jesus' acceptance of the limitations of humanity, his death, and his resurrection in order to restore our relationship with himself (Hebrews 2:14-18).

In all these ways, God is like us but at the same time, God is so different from us that we really cannot comprehend him. The Bible never uses the word "Trinity" but this is the term theologians use to express the unique way God exists. What we find in the Bible are very clear statements about God which, alone, make perfect sense but when taken together reveal just how different from us God really is—not just in his existence or in his character, as we've already seen, but in the way he exists.

The Bible teaches that the Father is God,[10] that Jesus is God,[11] and that the Holy Spirit is God.[12] Indeed, the three are referred to together by Jesus—in his command to baptize (Matthew 28:19) and in his promise of the Holy Spirit (John 14:26)—and in a variety of contexts by his apostles (2 Corinthians 13:14; 1 Peter 1:2; Jude 20-21).

Clearly, the Father is not the same person as Jesus ("the Son") or the Holy Spirit (Isaiah 42:1; Joel 2:28-29; Luke 3:21-22). Likewise, Jesus is not the same person as the Father or the Holy Spirit (John 11:41-42; 14:15-17; Acts 1:6-8). When Jesus prayed, he was not talking to himself. When he said he would send the Holy Spirit, he did not mean that he would return in a different form. As we have seen, all—the Father, the Son, and the Holy Spirit—are "God." Amazingly, however, the Bible is very clear that there is only one God (Deuteronomy 6:4; 1 Timothy 2:5).[13]

To fully understand the meaning of "Trinity," we first have to understand what it means to be a "person." We just observed several qualities of persons—they are real (vs. imaginary), they possess intellect, emotion, and will, they are self-aware, and they communicate, covenant, and love. In addition, a person is a

---

[10] Matthew 11:25; Romans 15:6; 1 Corinthians 8:4-6; Ephesians 4:6.
[11] Matthew 1:23; John 1:1; Hebrews 1:6, 8-9; 2 Peter 1:1.
[12] Acts 5:3-4; 1 Corinthians 12:4-7; 2 Peter 1:21.
[13] See also 1 Kings 8:60; Isaiah 45:21; John 17:3.

"centered self," i.e., a person is not a diffused presence, like a vapor, but has location. When Moses or Isaiah or John stood before God (Exodus 3:4-6; Isaiah 6:1; Revelation 4:2-3), they were aware that they were in the presence of a specific and very real person—a person who was fully and majestically present.

When we talk about the three persons of the Trinity, we must understand that each is wholly a person—the Father is a person, the Son is a person, and the Holy Spirit is a person. Each person is a unique "self-center," distinct from the others, with his (remember, gender does not apply to God) own intellect, will, and emotions. They all possess the same moral attributes. None is more divine than the others; they all are equally God, possessing all the attributes of deity.

As we try to understand the Trinity, it is common to wonder, "Then, is God one or is he three?" (A lot of people have drawn wrong conclusions, conclusions that deny clear teaching of the Scriptures, in attempting to answer that question.) The only biblical answer is that God is both one and three, depending on what we count. If we count persons, then (as we have seen) God is three—Father, Son, and Holy Spirit. If we count Gods (i.e., beings, or existences), however, he is one. Look at your hand. It is one hand but five fingers; whether it is one or five depends on what you count. The Trinity is the same, one existence but three persons.

You probably are thinking, I really don't understand this! Don't feel bad. That God is Trinity is not irrational, it just is another case where our understanding is limited by our experience. In our experience, every person has a separate existence. If God were to erase one member of our family—if he or she were to cease to exist—we would sense the loss but the family would survive, the rest of us would continue to exist. That's not the way it is with God. God is not a family, he is a Trinity.

In Trinity, the three persons of God—Father, Son (i.e., Jesus), and Holy Spirit—share a common existence. If anything happened so that Jesus ceased to exist, the entire Trinity would cease to exist. When Jesus died on the cross, he did not stop existing; he just died, like all of us will die someday, and he rose again to prove that he was very much alive. Death won't mark the end of our existence and it did not mark the end of his. Amazingly, however, when Jesus died for our sins, God—the one and only triune God—took death—the penalty for our sins—into himself.[14] Furthermore, when Jesus rose from the grave, the triune God demonstrated his triumph over death's threat of alienation and despair.

This concept of three persons sharing a single existence is so far beyond our experience that some see the Trinity as the ultimate proof of the truth of Biblical Christianity. Humans never would have thought of the concept of "Trinity" if it had not been revealed by God.

**Let's Talk About It**

- I once heard a preacher say, "One plus one plus one equals one; that's divine mathematics." What do you think of that statement? Why do you consider it helpful or mistaken?

- Since God is relationally complete within the Trinity—i.e., the Father, Son, and Holy Spirit relate, communicate, and love among themselves—he did not need to create. So, why did he? What motive would be strong enough to cause him to create other persons like himself? How would you support your conclusion from the Bible?

---

[14] It is not my intention, by this statement, to minimize the redemptive work of Christ. What I do want to underline is that the Father and the Spirit were not unaffected by Christ's atoning death. The doctrine of the Trinity teaches us, however, that the death of Jesus—the second person of the Trinity—entailed the acceptance of death into the Godhead. The eternal defeat of death ("the last enemy," 1 Corinthians 15:26), evidenced by Jesus' resurrection and ascension, was the triumph of the triune God over the forces of rebellion and alienation in his creation. By grace, he offers to include us in the victory he has won.

# CHAPTER 5

## God Reveals Himself

Since God is a relational person, it is not surprising that he has chosen to reveal himself to the humans whom he created. He loves us and desires relationship with us. Since relationship always requires communication and self-disclosure, God has taken the first step by revealing, in unmistakable ways, that he exists and that he is God.

God reveals himself through the things he does, including creation, history, and miracles. Inspired by the Holy Spirit, David sang, "The heavens declare the glory of God and the sky above proclaims his handiwork" (Psalm 19:1). As we saw in our first chapter, the ordered complexity of this physical world does not allow explanation on the basis of time-plus-chance alone. This universe testifies that it has a Maker. Paul is more specific; he states that "[God's] invisible attributes, namely, his eternal power and divine nature, have been clearly perceived ever since the creation of the world in the things that have been made" (Romans 1:20).

Although God's omnipotent power and absolute supremacy are invisible attributes, they are obvious to any thinking observer of the physical universe. The only rational conclusion is that an all-powerful God exists. Furthermore, from his ordering of his creation we see that this all-powerful God is good (i.e., loving, fair, and gracious); "he makes the sun rise on the evil and on the good, and sends rain on the just and on the unjust" (Matthew 5:45; cf. Acts 14:16-17).

Reflection on human history leads to the same conclusion. Human history is not random; it is directed by an all-wise God to accomplish his purpose of drawing us to himself. David suggests that God laughs at human efforts to direct the course of history (Psalm 2:1-4). His son, Solomon, compares the course of history to a stream of water that God guides with his hand as he chooses (Proverbs 21:1). Daniel testified to God's sovereignty in the course of nations, stating that God "removes kings and sets up kings" (Daniel 2:21). Nebuchadnezzar, one of the kings under whom Daniel served, experienced God's removal and reinstatement (Daniel 4:38-44). As a result, Nebuchadnezzar blessed God and acknowledged his sovereignty, saying,

> His dominion is an everlasting dominion, and his kingdom endures from generation to generation; all the inhabitants of the earth are accounted as nothing, and he does according to his will among the host of heaven and among the inhabitants of the earth; and none can stay his hand or say to him, 'What have you done?' (Daniel 4:34-35)

God also has shown his reality and his sovereign power by intervening in history at specific moments to do the otherwise impossible. We call these acts of God "miracles." When Israel was enslaved in Egypt, God delivered them by bringing ten plagues on Pharaoh and his people. Through Moses, God told Pharaoh that he had been placed on the throne of Egypt at this time "to show you my power, so that my name may be proclaimed in all the earth" (Exodus 9:16; see verses 13-15 for context; cf. Psalm 106:7-8). On Mount Carmel, God answered Elijah's prayer with a bolt of lightning to show that he alone is God (1 Kings 18:30-39).

Throughout the ministry of Jesus, God validated Jesus' claims to deity through many amazing miracles. Jesus, himself, appealed to his miracles as proof of the authenticity of his claims (John 10:24-25). John reports that Jesus did many other miracles that are not recorded "but these are written that you may believe that Jesus is the Christ, the Son of God, and that by believing you may have life in his name" (John 20:30-31).

At times we can see God's protecting and leading hand in our individual lives, as well. Although Joseph could have been angry with his brothers for selling him into slavery, he saw the hand of God in the events of his life. He told his brothers, "God sent me before you to preserve for you a remnant on earth and to keep alive for you many survivors. So it was not you who sent me here, but God" (Genesis 45:7-8). Paul told the Athenian philosophers that God determines the circumstances of all peoples "that they should seek

God, in the hope that they might find their way toward him and find him" (Acts 17:26-27).

God also has revealed his nature by creating humans to be like himself (Genesis 1:26-27). This means we can learn about God by looking at ourselves. Of course, we are sinful and God is not, so we must allow for the effects of sin on our human nature, but in fundamental ways we are like God and he is like us. Since we are rational, emotional, and relational persons with moral sensitivities, it is inconceivable that God should lack these attributes. (Paul appealed to this logic in his discussion with the philosophers of Athens [Acts 17:24-27].)

The best way to get to know a person, however, is to meet him. In Jesus, the eternal Second Person of the Trinity took the limitations of humanity and became one of us in order to show us God's character (John 1:14, 18). God entered our world as a helpless baby, lived his life in an occupied nation, faced life just as we do, modeled perfect holiness and service to others, accepted into himself the punishment of our sin, and rose triumphant over death and hell. Why would he do this? It is because God loves us (John 3:16). In order to have an intimate relationship with us, he became one of us.

God spoke through the Old Testament prophets "but in these last days he has spoken to us by his Son" (Hebrews 1:2). Jesus "is the radiance of the glory of God and the exact imprint of his nature" (Hebrews 1:3). Jesus told Philip, "Whoever has seen me has seen the Father" (John 14:9). Jesus "is the image of the invisible God" (Colossians 1:15), "for in him all the fullness of God was pleased to dwell, and to reconcile to himself all things, whether on earth or in heaven, making peace by the blood of his cross" (Colossians 1:19-20).

The disciples understood this. Peter testified, "we were eyewitnesses of his majesty" (2 Peter 1:16). John wrote, "the life was made manifest, and we have seen it, and testify to it and proclaim to you the eternal life, which was with the Father and was made manifest to us" (1 John 1:2). Thomas exclaimed, "My Lord and my God!" (John 20:28). If we want to know what God is like, the best thing we can do is look at Jesus.

We can observe the world God has created and see his hand in the history of nations and in the circumstances of our lives, but few of us have witnessed a miracle and none of us were alive when Jesus walked this earth. Furthermore, we may misinterpret God's acts or his self-revelation in Jesus. We are fortunate, therefore, that God has given us the Bible as the divinely authenticated record of his messages to humans.

Over and over in the Old Testament, the prophets claim that their message is from God (cf. Exodus 7:17; 2 Samuel 7:5; Isaiah 1:10-11; Jeremiah 2:5, and many, many other references). The New Testament apostles also claimed that the message they preached was from God (Acts 4:19-20; Galatians 1:11-12). The record of God's dealing with his people is given "for our instruction" (1 Corinthians 10:11).

In the Bible, we not only have a record of God's acts and words, we also have an authentic interpretation of their meaning. Paul wrote, "Christ died [that is history] for our sins [that is interpretation!]" (1 Corinthians 15:3). The Bible contains all that we need to live a life pleasing to God (2 Timothy 3: 15-17) and to experience intimacy with him. In the Bible we hear the voice of God today.

Sadly, not everyone has access to the Bible, but everyone can observe God's creation and can reflect on his or her own personality. That, alone, is sufficient to render a person "without excuse" (Romans 1:20). How much more accountable are we who have the Bible, and how blessed to hold in our hands God's message to us!

**Let's Talk About It**

- Which of the ways God reveals himself most powerfully leads you to worship his majesty? Describe an experience that illustrates this.

- Why do you suppose God reveals himself in multiple ways?

# CHAPTER 6

## How We Got the Bible

The story of how the Bible came to us over the centuries is fascinating. Its transmission (beginning from the time of Moses), the process by which Israel and the early church recognized the books of our Old and New Testaments, and God's often-miraculous protection of the Bible from rulers and radicals who attempted to destroy it makes an exciting story.

A history of Bible translations also is interesting. The earliest translation of the Old Testament books to Greek occurred about 150 B.C. Jerome translated the Bible into Latin about 390 A.D. The first translations of the Bible into ancient Middle Eastern languages are dated in the 5th Century and translation into modern European languages began in the 12th Century. Today, of course, there are many translations available.[15]

Even more foundational, however, is the record of God's revelation and affirmation of the Bible from the pages of Scripture, itself. That's the story we will examine in this chapter.

It is important to recognize that people—either individually or as a group—did not sit down to write the book we know today as the Bible. The Apostle Peter specifically rejects that suggestion:

> No prophecy of Scripture comes from someone's own interpretation. For no prophecy was ever produced by the will of man, but men spoke from God as they were carried along by the Holy Spirit. (2 Peter 1:20-21)

---

[15] A wonderful telling of this story can be found in Ralph Earle's 128 page book, *How We Got Our Bible* (3rd edition, Beacon Hill Press, 2010).

"Scripture"—the "writings" or "books" we know as the Bible—originated with God as he revealed his message to Hebrew prophets and apostles between 1,500 B.C. and A.D. 100.

Furthermore, Peter assures us that God did not take a chance that these prophets and apostles may have gotten it wrong. They were "carried along by the Holy Spirit." The Greek word translated "carried along" is the same word used by Luke to describe the four friends who "were bringing on a bed a man who was paralyzed" in order that Jesus might heal him (Luke 5:18). Peter uses this visual image to describe the full engagement of the Holy Spirit in the writing of Scripture. It is as if the Holy Spirit "carried" the writers to express in their words the meaning God intended.

There are a few places where God dictated to his prophets a message they were to communicate (cf. Exodus 34:27; Jeremiah 36:2) but even when the prophets and apostles wrote history or poetry or letters of admonition and instruction, the words that they wrote carried the meaning God intended—they were God's words. The writers "spoke from God as they were carried along by the Holy Spirit." God the Holy Spirit so directed the thoughts of the writers of Scripture that they were kept from error and were guided to express God's message with perfect accuracy.

Paul uses a different word to describe God's role in giving us the Bible. He wrote:

> All Scripture is breathed out by God and profitable for teaching, for reproof, for correction, and for training in righteousness, that the man of God may be competent, equipped for every good work. (2 Timothy 3:16-17)

The Greek word for "breathed out" was rendered by King James' translators as "inspired," so God's role in giving us an accurate and trustworthy record of his revelation often is referred to as "the doctrine of inspiration." Just as our breath powers our speech, so the Scriptures are the very voice of God to us.

Note, too, that Paul—carried along by the Holy Spirit—does not limit this affirmation to certain passages, teachings, or modes of revelation; he asserts that "all Scripture" is God breathed. God intends that by building our lives on his Word, the Bible, we should be "equipped for every good work."

This was understood clearly by Jesus' disciples and leaders of the 1st Century church. Peter introduced quotations from Psalm 69:25 and Psalm 109:8 by saying, "the Scriptures had to be fulfilled which the Holy Spirit spoke beforehand by the mouth of David" (Acts 1:16). Thus, Peter recognized that the words of David's psalms were spoken by God the Holy Spirit. Paul also recognized that the words of Isaiah, the prophet, were spoken by God (Acts 28:25).

The Holy Spirit's superintendence of the words of Scripture was not limited to the Old Testament writings, however; he also inspired— or "carried along"—the New Testament writers. Thus, Peter refers to the writings of Paul as having value and as being subject to distortion like "the other [i.e., Old Testament] Scriptures" (2 Peter 3:16).[16] Paul also quotes Luke's record of a statement by Jesus as having equal authority with God's revelation to Moses (1 Timothy 5:18; cf. Deuteronomy 25:4 and Luke 10:7). Clearly, the Apostles and the early church considered the New Testament books just as truly the word of God as the books of the Old Testament.

Some theologians propose various criteria for deciding what parts of the Bible are authoritative and what parts can be ignored as irrelevant for us today. For much of the 20th Century, liberal theologians applied the test of modern science. If a passage could be understood and explained within the naturalistic frame of modern science, it was accepted as accurate; if not, it was "reinterpreted" in ways consistent with the "modern" world-view. Thus, the Bible was freed from all references to the supernatural, including prophecy, miracle, and resurrection from the dead.

More recently, some who claim to be "Evangelical" have proposed other criteria, such as "Jesus Christ," for determining what is essential and what can be considered less important or even dismissed. In doing so, however, like liberal theologians of the 20th Century, they place their own judgment above that of the Holy Spirit who inspired the biblical writers. They decide what promotes Christ and regard as less important passages they conclude do not promote Christ. Rather than accepting all of God's word as equally inspired and authoritative, they decide what is authoritative and what can be dismissed.

---

[16] The word translated "other" is *loipos* (λοιπός), which clearly means "the rest" or "others of the same kind." Greek has another word (*alla*, ἀλλά) that means "others of a different or contrasting kind."

It is extremely important, therefore, to observe how Jesus regarded the Scriptures. Jesus refers to the Scriptures as "the commandment of God" (Mark 7:9) and "the word of God" (Mark 7:13). He taught that "Scripture cannot be broken" (John 10:35) and that "until heaven and earth pass away, not an iota, not a dot, will pass from the Law until all is accomplished" (Matthew 5:18). Jesus did not discriminate between the various literary genre or modes of revelation; all is God's word and all will be accomplished. Furthermore, Jesus' confidence in Scripture extended to the finest detail of the script. The smallest letter of the Greek alphabet is the iota and the smallest mark in the Hebrew alphabet is the keraia (κεράια, translated "dot" or "horn"), roughly equivalent to the mark that distinguishes a capital Q from a capital O in English. In saying this, Jesus went out of his way to affirm the trustworthiness of the finest details of the Scriptures.

Jesus' confidence in Scripture was not limited to the written script, however, it also included the grammar of the text. In his response to the Sadducees' question about resurrection, Jesus' case turns on the tense of a verb, the fact that the verb "I am" is present tense rather than past tense (Matthew 22:32). Furthermore, Jesus states that the Sadducees' question reveals that they "know neither the Scriptures nor the power of God" (Matthew 22:29; see verses 23-33 for context).

That must have come as a stinging rebuke to these religious scholars but on another occasion Jesus said something similar to two of his disciples. In his post-resurrection appearance on the road to Emmaus, Jesus responded to a tentative account of reports of his resurrection by saying,

> Oh foolish ones, and slow of heart to believe all that the prophets have spoken! Was it not necessary that the Christ should suffer these things and enter into his glory? (Luke 24:25-26)

Imagine how they must have felt to have been called "foolish." And, what indicated their folly? It was the fact that they failed to believe all that the prophets had spoken. Since Jesus' life and death and resurrection had been prophesied in Scripture, its fulfillment was so certain as to be considered "necessary."

I would have loved to have been a companion with those disciples, that day, when Jesus, "beginning with Moses and all the Prophets, interpreted to them in all the Scriptures the things concerning himself" (Luke 24:27). As they reflected on that experience, those disciples asked, "Did not our hearts burn within us while he talked to us on the road, while he opened to us the Scriptures?" (Luke 22:32).

Later that evening, Jesus appeared to the sequestered disciples back in Jerusalem and said to them, "These are my words [or message] that I spoke to you while I was still with you, that everything written about me in the Law of Moses and the Prophets and the Psalms must be fulfilled" (Luke 22:44). Whereas the Christian Scriptures are divided into two sections, the Old Testament and the New Testament, the Hebrew Scriptures, then and today, are divided into three sections: first, the books of Moses (i.e., the first five books, known as "The Law"), then "The Prophets" (Isaiah, Jeremiah, Ezekiel, and the twelve Minor Prophets, plus Joshua, Judges, 1 and 2 Samuel, and 1 and 2 Kings), and finally, "The Writings" (Psalms, Proverbs, Job, Song of Solomon, Ruth, Lamentations, Ecclesiastes, Esther, Daniel, Ezra, Nehemiah, and 1 and 2 Chronicles, known popularly as "The Psalms," since Psalms was the first and largest book in this third section). So, it were as if Jesus affirmed the accuracy and authority of Scripture "from cover to cover."

If that was Jesus' view of the Bible, what should ours be? Are we wiser than he?

## Let's Talk About It

- Why is Jesus' view of the Bible so significant for you and me? How would you respond to the questions in the paragraph above?

- Does this mean there are no "problem passages" that challenge our understanding of the Bible? What do you do with statements in the Bible that appear to conflict with other passages or that appear at odds with our 21st Century scientific understandings?

# CHAPTER 7

## God's Image in Us

What makes us special? Many, of course, say humans are not particularly special other than that we are a little more advanced than other inhabitants of this planet. Those who take their cues from the Bible, however, affirm that humans are very special. God created humans for "eternal life"—an unending relationship of intimacy with himself (John 3:16; 6:40; 17:3).

As to what makes humans special, what differentiates us from the rest of God's creation, however, there is more confusion. Some have contended that the thing that sets humans apart is that they have a soul. The Bible does affirm that humans have "soul"; Genesis 2:7 states that "God breathed into his nostrils the breath of life, and the man [Adam] became a living creature." (The words "living creature" translate the Hebrew word for "soul.") The same word is used, however, of animals that God created to populate the sea and land (Genesis 1:21, 24), so "soul" cannot be the thing that differentiates us from the rest of creation.

Others have contended that "spirit," rather than "soul," differentiates us from the animal kingdom. In both Hebrew and Greek, the word for "spirit" also means "breath." Thus, Genesis 2:7, quoted above, may be understood to teach that God gave Adam "spirit." Also in the context of the creation narrative, however, God lists those that have "the breath of life" as including "every beast of the earth and every bird of the heavens and everything that creeps on the earth" (Genesis 1:30; cf. 7:22). That doesn't support the suggestion that spirit ("the breath of life") is unique to humans either.

The one thing that is unique to humans is God's choice to create humans "in his own image"[17] (Genesis 1:26-27), but what does that mean? What is the image of God in us? The Bible never defines "the image of God" but we are safe to assume that it includes all those ways in which humans are uniquely like God and different from the animals.

There are ways in which we are not like God. Each human exists individually; we are not trinities. Also, unlike God, humans have physical bodies;[18] we don't look like God and God does not look like us.

On the other hand, there are significant ways in which we are like God. Like God, we are personal beings—we are rational (able to think and to know), emotional (able to experience joy, sorrow, anger, and delight and to empathize with others), volitional (able to make meaningful choices), potent (able to act in ways that change our environment), and relational (able to communicate, to love, and to covenant). Our capacities in all these areas are not equal to God's capacities—ours are limited whereas his are infinite—but they are like his. Similarly, like God, we are moral; we have the ability to recognize the difference between right and wrong (good and evil) and to choose which we will pursue. God is holy—he invariably chooses what is right; even though we are sinful, he desires that we should be holy (1 Peter 1:14-16) and has created us as moral persons, like himself.

There is another way in which God has made us like himself. Jesus told us that "God is Spirit" (John 4:24).[19] What does that mean? What does it mean to be "spirit"?

Certainly, a spiritual being is personal and moral, as noted above. As such, spiritual beings are able to relate to God and to enjoy his presence. Simply physical beings (e.g., animals) may be capable of basic communication on a physical plane but they do not have the ability to establish spiritual relationships. This is possible only for spiritual beings. Because humans are spiritual as well as physical

---

[17] Theologians often refer to the image of God in humans by the Latin expression, *imago dei*.

[18] When the Second Person of the Trinity came to redeem us, he took a body like ours, but that is not the way he existed from eternity past.

[19] The word *pneuma* ($\pi\nu\varepsilon\hat{\upsilon}\mu\alpha$) is the same one translated above as "breath," but here—and in other contexts—it has a more specific meaning. It refers to a person that does not have a physical body. Thus, it is used here of God, but it also is used of angels (e.g., Hebrews 1:13-14), of demons (e.g., Matthew 8:16), and of the Third Person of the Trinity (e.g., John 14:26).

beings, those who love God experience an intimate relationship with him. God "abides" (or lives) in them and they "abide" in God (1 John 4:15).

Another way in which God has created humans like himself is that we are immortal—we will live forever. God has revealed that death is not the end for us. Every human continues to exist after death and each will be held accountable for the thing she or he has done (Revelation 20:11-13). God is eternal. God has existed from the infinite past and he will exist into the infinite future. We are not eternal. Unlike God, our existence has a beginning, but like him, we will exist into the infinite future. That's what it means to be immortal. We are not eternal but we are immortal; we are not the same as God but we are like him.

Every human being bears God's image. This is the basis for capital punishment for murder (Genesis 9:6) and it exposes the inappropriateness of degrading our fellow human while piously praising God (James 3:8-9). When we denigrate, abuse, or oppress another person we offend God, whose image she or he bears (Proverbs 14:31).

Perhaps more important than understanding the meaning of the image of God in us is the motive that moved God to create us like himself. I have observed that God desires an intimate relationship with us, that the only explanation why God created anything is his desire to expand the circle of his relationships. To do that, it was necessary for him to create others who not only could experience his love but who could love him in return. God's choice to expand the circle of his relationships required him to create others like himself. This he did when he created our first parents. Irrespective of our sin—however awful—we continue to bear his image and, as a result, redemption and intimacy with God is possible for all of us.

### Let's Talk About It

- How do you respond to the suggestion that God made you like himself so that you could experience an intimate relationship with God for the rest of eternity?

- How does the fact that all humans share God's image shape the way I should relate to others in my life?

# CHAPTER 8

## What About Gender?

Historically, discussion among theologians did not assign much attention to the question of gender but changes in Western culture have made gender an important topic. As we shall see, neglect of the topic by theologians in the past has not been for lack of attention to gender in the Scriptures. In eternal perspective, the issue of gender may be moot[20] but as long as we are male and female, gender is an important topic regarding which the Bible has much to say.

After creating humans "male and female," God declared his creation—including our sexuality—to be "very good" (Genesis 1:31). Like all appetites, our sexual appetite must be disciplined. Specifically, God has provided that sexual desires should be satisfied within the context of a life-long union between one man and one woman (1 Corinthians 7:2). God commands that marriage should be honored, affirming that sex within marriage is pure and holy (Hebrews 13:4). Sex outside of marriage—pre-marital, extra-marital "affairs," and homosexual lifestyles—are forbidden in Scripture (1 Thessalonians 4:3-4; Exodus 20:14; Matthew 5:28; Leviticus 18:22).[21] God also cautions Christian husbands and wives against denying one another access to sexual fulfillment, except for devotional prayer and then only by agreement and only briefly

---

[20] Jesus said that "in the resurrection [i.e., in the new bodies we will receive for eternity] they neither marry nor are given in marriage, but are like angels in heaven" (Matthew 22:30). This suggests that gender distinctions are not eternal.
[21] In biblical perspective, a critical distinction exists between temptation and behavior that represents a choice to yield to a temptation. Thus, in the case of homosexuality, it is the behavior, rather than same sex attraction, which God condemns (Romans 1:18-32). Someone who understands this and has appropriated God's grace to live a life of purity despite his same sex attraction is Wesley Hill. I have found most helpful his book, *Washed and Waiting: Reflections on Christian Faithfulness and Homosexuality* (Grand Rapids: Zondervan, 2010).

(1 Corinthians 7:3-5). Children, furthermore, are a blessing from the Lord which husband and wife share (Psalm 127:3; 1 Peter 3:7).

Western culture, today, seems intent on erasing the male-female distinction and on legitimizing—even privileging—alternative sexual behavior and identities. This should not surprise us, since the Bible warns of an erosion of morals before Christ returns (2 Timothy 3:1-5; Matthew 24:12).

In considering the significance of gender from a Christian perspective, the first truth is that men and women stand equal before God. God created humans "male and female" and, together, commanded them to "be fruitful and multiply and fill the earth and subdue it and have dominion over...every living thing that moves on the earth" (Genesis 1:27-28).

Within the Christian community it often is suggested that the creation account in Genesis 2 establishes the subordinate role of women because Eve is given to Adam as "a helper fit [or suited, or appropriate] for him" (Genesis 2:18, 20). That reflects a misunderstanding of the text, however. The same term, "helper," is applied repeatedly in the Old Testament to God (Psalm 10:14; 54:4; 118:7; Hosea 13:9). No one understands these passages to suggest that God is subordinate to his people.

In the New Testament, Paul states clearly that men and women are interdependent (1 Corinthians 11:11-12) and, in marriage, that the needs of husbands and wives deserve equal consideration (1 Corinthians 7:3-5). Peter notes that women may be physically weaker than their husbands but they are equal partners—"heirs with you of the grace of life" (1 Peter 3:7). It would be difficult to argue from these verses that either men or women are less valued in God's sight.

We might wonder how the apostles came to a perspective that was so counter-cultural in their day. 1st Century Hebrew culture was patriarchal and women lacked many of the privileges owned by men. Sadly, furthermore, women often were devalued. Jesus, however, set a very different example. Whereas women may have been ignored by others, Jesus frequently ministered to women. He healed Peter's mother-in-law (Luke 4:38-39), restored life to the son of a widowed mother (Luke 7:11-15), and healed a woman with a hemorrhage and who, thus, was ceremonially "unclean" (Luke 8:43-48). Jesus also raised a little girl from death to life (Luke

8:41-42, 49-56), healed a woman with scoliosis (Luke 13:10-13), and rescued an adulterous woman from public stoning (John 8:3-11). In addition, Jesus allowed a sinful woman to anoint his feet (Luke 7:36-38) and he initiated and pursued conversation with a Samaritan woman who was shunned by her community (John 4:7-30).

Jesus highlighted women in his parables as positive examples. Jesus points to a woman who celebrates a find as a picture of heavenly joy (Luke 15:8-10). He commends a woman who would not give up as an encouragement to persistent prayer (Luke 18:1-8). He also receives the lavish worship by Mary as an example for others (John 12:1-8).

Mary and Martha, with their brother, Lazarus, were counted by Jesus as special friends whom he visited regularly (Luke 10:38-42; John 11:5-6, 17-45; 12:1-3). Matthew tells us that "many women" were among those who followed Jesus (Matthew 27:55) and Luke notes that there were women who financially supported Jesus' ministry (Luke 8:2-3). When Jesus rose from the dead, he appeared first not to the disciples but to a group of women (Matthew 28:1-10; Mark 16:9-10; John 20:1-2, 11-18). Clearly, Jesus valued women; his attitude toward and treatment of women was very counter-cultural.

There are two places where the value accorded to women historically has been diminished among Christians; one is in the marriage relationship and the other is in the church. Some teach that the Bible requires wives to live in submission to their husbands and that husbands have the right and responsibility to rule their wives. Paul did write, "Wives, submit to your own husbands, as to the Lord" (Ephesians 5:22), but this verse—like all verses in the Bible—must be read in context. Taken out of context, this Scripture has been misinterpreted and abused.

Ephesians 5:22 occurs in a passage (Ephesians 5:21-6:9) in which Paul discusses relationships within the Christian community, including the relationship of husbands and wives, of parents and children, and of masters and slaves (or, in today's economy, of employers and employees). Paul opens his comments on relationships by asserting that "submission" is to be mutual within the Christian community (Ephesians 5:21).

Within marriage, wives are to submit to their husbands but husbands also are to submit to their wives. "Love"—the biblical obligation of husbands (Ephesians 5:25, 28)—is a form of submission, since it entails privileging the good of the other over one's own good. Furthermore, the commands to love and respect (Ephesians 5:33) address the specific temptations and needs of men and women. Men need to be respected. Sin produces self-doubts and insecurities to which men naturally respond with physical dominance, aggression, and violence that can lead to spousal abuse. Respect addresses a man's insecurities, and enables wholesome relationships. Women need to be loved. Sin produces self-doubts and insecurities to which women naturally respond with assertive self-protection. A loving, caring relationship addresses a woman's insecurities.

Paul's statement that "the husband is the head of the wife even as Christ is the head of the church" (Ephesians 5:23) is especially prone to misunderstanding. Clearly, to be "head" does not mean ruler (as it is often interpreted), since Paul began teaching in this section by admonishing mutual submission. It is more consistent to understand "headship" as "source," and thus a function of responsibility, rather than prerogative. We should note how Paul describes Christ's "headship" of the church. Christ "is himself its Savior" (Ephesians 5:23). "Christ loved the church and gave himself up for her" (Ephesians 5:25). Christ "nourishes and cherishes" the church (Ephesians 5:29). This is not a description of hierarchal leadership but of self-giving love.

This does not mean that husbands and fathers are exempt from leadership within their families but it does indicate how leadership is to be exercised. Husbands are to love their wives and children are to obey their parents (Ephesians 6:1). The writer of Hebrews admonishes readers, "obey your leaders and submit to them" (Hebrews 13:17a). Although the marriage relationship is not specifically in view in this passage, the rationale given for submission may be instructive. Readers are reminded that their leaders "keep watch over your souls, as those who will have to give an account" (Hebrews 13:17b). A leaderless family is not a healthy family; Christian men need to accept responsibility for leadership in their homes. Their leadership, however, should be loving, nourishing, and self-sacrificing, always exercised with awareness that God holds the husband accountable for the health of his marriage and his family. Recognizing this, furthermore, can make it easier for a woman to yield to her husband at times when their perspectives differ.

The other context in which the value accorded to women has been diminished is in the church. This is particularly anomalous since Jesus so clearly valued women. Nevertheless, some of the most difficult Bible passages to interpret are those that speak to the issue of the role of women in the church. Whenever we need to interpret a difficult passage, it is important first to establish clear teachings of Scripture that bear on the topic.

When God sent the Holy Spirit, on the Feast of Pentecost, Peter announced the fulfillment of Joel's prophecy (cf. Joel 2:28-32):

> In the last days it shall be, God declares, that I will pour out my Spirit on all flesh and your sons and your daughters shall prophesy and your young men shall see visions, and your old men shall dream dreams; even on my male servants and female servants in those days I will pour out my Spirit and they shall prophesy. (Acts 2:17-18)

Whereas the Old Testament had privileged a male priesthood, Peter affirms the new era purchased by Christ and inaugurated by the Spirit would be blessed with trans-generational leadership, inclusive of both men and women.

The place of women in the family, in the church, and in the community goes right to the heart of the Gospel. Paul states this repeatedly, although nowhere more clearly than in his letter to the Galatian Christians.

> Now that faith has come we are no longer under a guardian, for in Christ Jesus you are all sons of God, through faith. For as many of you as were baptized into Christ have put on Christ. There is neither Jew nor Greek, there is neither slave nor free, there is neither male nor female, for you are all one in Christ Jesus. (Galatians 3:25-28; cf. Colossians 3:11)

The fundamental principle is this: The Gospel removes divisions and barriers, it does not erect them (Ephesians 2:11-22). The Gospel eliminates distinctions that we, as sinful people, set up among us—ethnic, economic, and gender—and treats all as equals in God's sight.

Passages most often cited to exclude women from ministries of leadership and teaching in the church include 1 Corinthians 11:2-16, 1 Corinthians 14:34-35, and 1 Timothy 2:8-15. Recall that when interpreting a difficult passage, it is important first to remind ourselves of clear teachings of Scripture that bear on the topic.

Because God's truth is consistent, when any passage appears to contradict the clear teaching of other Scripture, we must assume that our initial reading is mistaken and search for a less obvious interpretation (i.e., less obvious to us, shaped as we are by our language and culture) in keeping with the broader teaching of Scripture.

1 Corinthians 11:2-16 contains difficulties for all biblical interpreters. Clearly, Paul has cultural norms in mind since he appeals to some hair styles and lengths as "disgraceful" (verses 5-6, 14-15). His reference to "the angels" (verse 10) most likely refers to "messengers" (the common meaning of the word used) or teachers in the local congregation who share the expectations and mores of the broader culture, rather than to supernatural beings. As already noted, the meaning of "head" is not "ruler" but "source," and thus establishes responsibility. If there is a transcultural application of this passage, it must be that men and women are interdependent and equal, as previously noted.

It may be that the tradition of synagogue meetings, with men and women on opposite sides of the room, is reflected in 1 Corinthians 14:34-35. Inasmuch as women in the Roman Empire did not enjoy the educational opportunities available to men, these realities may be reflected in Paul's teaching about women in the church. Thus, Paul's concern is not for gender restriction but for decorum (cf. verses 39-40). Less educated women should not shout questions to their husbands during the service. Whether or not this was the context of Paul's instruction, it seems clear that Paul did not intend to lay down a general prohibition against women.

Finally, in 1 Timothy 2:8-15, Paul's concern also is for propriety in public worship—men should avoid "anger or quarreling" and women should dress modestly (verses 8-10). The next verses (11-12) state that women should not teach but it is important to note the rationale for this instruction. Paul notes that "Adam was formed first, then Eve" (verse 13). That cannot be taken as a case for the superiority of Adam since, in Genesis 1, the animals were created before Adam. If anything is to be deduced from the order of creation, it would be that woman, having been created last, is the crowning glory of God's creative activity—the completion of man (cf. 1 Corinthians 11:7). Paul also notes that "Adam was not deceived, but the woman was deceived and became a transgressor" (verse 14). Again, the evidence Paul presents appears to argue against the subordination of women. Eve was "deceived" but Adam, who had been instructed by God (Genesis 2:16-17), sinned knowingly; thus

Adam's culpability was greater than Eve's. That is not a case for prohibiting women from speaking in church. It could, however, be a basis for prohibiting those who are uninstructed from assuming leadership. Since many women in the 1st Century had limited educational opportunities, as noted above, that could explain Paul's restriction on their appointment to teaching roles. Verse 15 assures these women that their role as mother and homemaker is spiritually significant, even though they may not be qualified to teach. Nevertheless, the rule in this passage should not be generalized outside of the context in which it was given.

If there is any doubt about Paul's attitude regarding the place of women in the church, we need only observe his practice. Priscilla and Aquila traveled with Paul from Corinth to Ephesus (Acts 18:18-19). The order of names is significant since, in 1st Century culture, first place was given to the leader. That Priscilla was accompanied by her husband assures that relationships were chaste, but there is no doubt that Priscilla was the principle teacher of the two. This is evident again in the report of Priscilla and Aquila's instruction of Apollos (Acts 18:26). Note, too, that Priscilla's teaching ministry was not limited to teaching other women.

By the end of Paul's third missionary journey, despite restrictions on women in the broader culture, apparently there were many women in leadership roles in the church. In Romans 16, Paul urges the church in Rome to welcome "our sister Phoebe, a servant of the church at Cenchreae" (verses 1-2) and sends greetings and commendations to "Prisca" (a shortened form of Priscilla—verse 3), to Mary (verse 6), to Junia (verse 7), to Tryphaena (verse 12), to the mother of Rufus (verse 13), and to Julia (verse 15). It is inconceivable that Paul would include all of these women in his ministry if, in fact, he prohibited women from leadership roles on the basis of gender.

As we have seen, women and men stand equal in God's sight. They are called to mutual submission, although God holds husbands and fathers accountable for the physical provision and spiritual health of their families. Wives, as equal partners of the grace of life, are the glory of their husbands, his completion and colleague (i.e., appropriate helper). No other religion accords to women the high status they hold in Biblical Christianity. For this we all praise God!

**Let's Talk About It**

- In view of the attention and respect that Jesus and Paul extended to women, how do you account for the suppression of women within so many Christian communities? Is this part of a larger pattern of discrimination and disrespect? Where else do you see this evidenced? How do you respond to the unbiblical patterns and behaviors you see?

- What implications of a biblical understanding of gender do you see for relationships within your family? If you are single, what implications do you see for your relationships with others? If you are married (or expect to be married), what expectations do you hold for yourself and your spouse that you need to discuss together?

# CHAPTER 9

## Why Life is Tough

No doubt you've noticed that life is tough. Things often do not go the way we would like. Disagreements too often turn into fights and, when nations fight, it's all-out war. People get hurt and people hurt other people. Worst of all, people die. There are few things that hurt more than when we lose someone we love. Maybe you've wondered why life is so tough. Why can't people just be nice? Why does so much bad stuff happen? If God loves us so much, why is life so hard?

The Bible assures us that God does love us. Furthermore, the Bible tells us that God created the first humans perfect and placed them in a perfect garden. He said that everything he created was "very good" (Genesis 1:31). Sadly, our first parents (and each of us since) rebelled against the God who created them, asserted their independence, and chose what they thought was best for them instead of accepting that their loving God knows what is best. (Sound familiar? It should. Don't we all think we know what's best for ourselves, often rejecting God's clear instructions?) The Bible calls this "sin."

There are many ways to define sin. We could study the character of God and then note that sin is all that is opposite to God's character. We could study the lives of those who are identified in the Bible as sinners. Or we could list those things which are called sins in the Scriptures. A very good way, however, is to study the words for sin which are used in the New Testament.

The word for sin which occurs more often than any other in the New Testament (*hamartia*, ἁμαρτία—more than 265 times in its various forms) literally means "to miss the mark." In classical Greek, the term was commonly used of an inaccurate spearman and it occurs often in this sense. The picture is that of a person whose duty is to lodge his spear right in the center of a target but who, due to some fault—whether inherited handicap, lack of skill, lack of care, or deliberate negligence—misses the mark. The picture is appropriate, for God's character is the moral standard for us as humans. If we are to experience intimacy with him, our character must conform to his. He is just and righteous and loving and perfectly trustworthy and he calls us to be like himself. If we are to be acceptable to God, it is necessary to perfectly attain God's standard.

The only person who did not miss the mark—who actually committed no sin—was Jesus (1 Peter 2:21-22). Everyone else, from Adam and Eve to you and me, has missed the mark of God's holiness (Romans 3:23). The ultimate result of missing the mark is death (James 1:15). It's just a reality; everyone (except Jesus) has sinned and therefore deserves to die. Obviously, that is not what God intended and it's not what we want.

If a spearman missed his target during practice, he might be disqualified by his commanding officer. If he missed his target during battle, he might be killed. As persons who have missed God's target for us, our situation is very serious, too. Trying to be good is fruitless (Mark 10:18; Romans 3:10-12). Religious ritual and sacrifices also are of no help; "it is impossible for the blood of bulls and goats to take away sins" (Hebrews 10:4). Thankfully, there is a remedy for us who have missed the mark. The good news ("gospel") is that "Christ died for our sins" (1 Corinthians 15:3). The punishment we deserve for missing the mark—i.e., eternal separation from a holy God—already has been paid!

A second word for "sin" used in the New Testament (*paraptoma*, παράπτωμα) is made from the root of the word "to fall." (The same root is used for a dead body—i.e., one who has fallen.) A literal translation of the word would be "to fall aside." The picture which the word suggests is that of a runner who stumbles and collapses by the side of the track when he should have finished the race. Thus, when used to describe sin, it suggests the complete failure of humans to measure up to the high standard which God requires. It is not that humans have failed to do well enough to attain God's approval; we have not even been able to complete what is required. We have "fallen aside" when we should have completed the course.

For some reason I do not understand, the common translation for this word in our English Bibles is "trespass." The word "trespass" means without permission to enter or pass across property that rightfully belongs to someone else. Frankly, "trespass" doesn't seem to me to be a word that expresses very well the meaning "to fall aside," but this is the English word that commonly is used. Nevertheless, it often is helpful to realize that "trespass" should be understood as "to fall aside."

Jesus cautions us to forgive those who "fall aside" if we expect God to forgive us when we "fall aside" (Matthew 6:14-15). Likewise, Paul urges the Galatian Christians to restore those who "fall aside" (Galatians 6:1). Just as "missing the mark" leads to death, "falling aside" also leaves us dead. Through the death of Christ, however, "God made [us] alive together with him [i.e., Jesus], having forgiven all of our trespasses [i.e., every occasion on which we have fallen aside]" (Colossians 2:13; see vv. 13-15).

A third word which is used frequently for "sin" in the New Testament (*adikia*, ἀδικία) seems to stress the wickedness of sin. It is really a compound word—the prefix of denial is attached to the root meaning "right." Literally, it means "not right," or perhaps "un-right," and thus, wicked or evil. Usually the word is translated in the King James Version as "unrighteousness," but more recent translations use various English words. When Jesus tells us there is no "un-right" in God (John 7:18), the English Standard Version translates the word "falsehood." When John writes that "all wrongdoing is sin [i.e., missing the mark]" (1 John 5:17), the word translated "wrongdoing" is "un-right." Pursuit of "un-right" is serious. Paul warns Roman Christians that "for those who are self-seeking and do not obey the truth, but obey unrighteousness ["un-right"], there will be wrath and fury" (Romans 2:8).

A fourth New Testament word which emphasizes the wrongness of sin and our guilt before God (*parabasis*, παράβασις) means, literally, "to step over the line." The word originates in an athletic context. You know that many sports have boundary lines. If one steps "out of bounds," a penalty is imposed. It is the same with us. God has set limits to be observed if we are to experience intimacy with him. If we do not—if we step over the line—then we are guilty before God. The English word most often used to translate this Greek word is "transgression."

The significance of "stepping over the line" helps us understand the seriousness of sin. James notes that it takes only one occasion of "stepping over the line" to incur guilt (James 2:11). In a phrase that often is misunderstood, Paul points out that if no line is drawn, stepping over it is not an issue (Romans 4:15); nevertheless, those who lived before the law was given (i.e., before the boundary lines were drawn) were sinners like the rest of us.

Another word used for sin in the New Testament (*anomia*, ἀνομία) emphasizes our disobedience to God. This also is a compound word; in this word the prefix of denial is attached to the word "law." The word which results does not mean that there is no law, but rather that the person is acting in rebellion against the law which God has made. We might translate it as "anti-law," but the more common translation found in the New Testament is "lawlessness." Since the law is a reflection of God's character, rebellion against God's law is rebellion against God himself.

This theme of rebellious violation of God and his law is common when this word is used. Peter, on the day of Pentecost, declared that his listeners had "crucified and killed [Jesus] by the hands of lawless men" (Acts 2:23). John defines sin ("missing the mark") not as a simple mistake but as rebellion against God and his law (1 John 3:4). The writer of Hebrews quotes Psalm 45 to describe Jesus' character and values: "You have loved righteousness and hated wickedness ['anti-law']" (Hebrews 1:9).

The last word commonly used for "sin" in the New Testament (*apeitheia*, ἀπᾲθεια) also emphasizes the rebelliousness of sin. Literally, the word means "not able to be persuaded," or we might say, "hard-headed." The problem is not that people do not know what God requires but that we are "hard-headed" and refuse to accept that which God has revealed to us. The result of our hard-headed rebellion is that we are disobedient to God. It is for this reason, I suppose, that this word usually is translated "disobedience."

The writer of Hebrews uses this word to explain why the generation of Israelites who escaped from Egypt died in the wilderness; it was "because of disobedience" (Hebrews 4:6)—because of their hard-headed refusal to receive the good news of God's gift of the Promised Land. Paul contrasts the receptivity of the Gentile nations with hard-headed refusal of ancient Israel to respond to God's invitation to relationship and intimacy (Romans 10:20-21). When writing to Christians in Ephesus, Paul refers to those who live in sin as "sons of disobedience [hard-headedness]" (Ephesians 5:6) and states that God's anger (appropriately) is directed toward them.

Because English has just one word for "sin," it is easy for us to miss the nuances that fill out the significance of this concept in the New Testament. Sin is not just "sin," it is "missing the mark," "falling aside" instead of completing what is required, wicked "un-right," "stepping over the line" in violation of God's character, an "anti-law" attitude and disposition, and "rebellious hard-headedness." Any inclination we may have to minimize the seriousness of sin is dashed by a study of the words used by God's inspired authors of the New Testament.

So, life is tough because we rebelled against God, resulting in alienation from him, from one another, and from ourselves. Our only encouragement lies in the fact that Jesus took our sin into himself, paid its penalty, and offers us his righteousness (1 Peter 2:24; 2 Corinthians 5:21). He offers to heal our alienation and invites us into intimacy with himself. What an amazing God!

**Let's Talk About It**

- As you reflect on the various words the New Testament writers use to describe sin, what impresses you?

- Why does our culture often minimize the seriousness of sin? Why do we also see this tendency in ourselves?

# CHAPTER 10

## Our Special Home

The beauty of the earth has inspired artists and poets for millennia and brings joy to all of us. The diversity of ecosystems, from arctic tundra to desert flowers to tropical jungles is amazing! Mountains, lakes, rivers, waterfalls, oceans, rock-walled cliffs, forests, and plains drive tourist industries and invite seekers of beauty and novelty. This is an amazing world in which we live! (Yes, there are ugly places too, but most of those were created by humans.)

To our knowledge, this planet also is unique. In light of the millions of galaxies and billions of planets in the universe, it seems incredible that only one inhabited world exists. That improbability justifies (in the minds of many) the drive to discover other inhabited worlds but, to date, we have found none. I doubt that we ever will. The underlying motivation for much of the scientific search for other worlds seems to be a desire to disprove the uniqueness of our special home and of our existence as intelligent, relational beings.

The Bible simply asserts that "God created the heavens and the earth" (Genesis 1:1). To ask why God created is to probe deeply into the mind of God. He certainly did not create because he had to; God is the eternally existing one—the only eternally existing one. In no way is he dependent on his creation. Nevertheless, at some point in eternity past, our personal, relational, and loving God freely chose to expand the circle of the relationships that existed eternally within the Trinity by creating others like himself with whom he could share that relationship. Why he would choose to do so is, perhaps, the ultimate mystery of all time. That he chose to do so is affirmed by Scripture (Ephesians 1:3-6) and is evidenced by our very existence.

We may find clues to this mystery by asking what it is that brings God pleasure. God does not take pleasure in the death of the wicked but he is pleased when the wicked repent and turn to him (Ezekiel 33:11). God is delighted when people choose his ways, when they are faithful, loving, just, and righteous (Jeremiah 9:24). The Psalmist tells us that God takes pleasure in his people (Psalm 149:4), in those who respect, honor, and love him (Psalm 147:11). Jesus said that God delights to give "the kingdom" (i.e., his reign in their lives) to those who trust him (Luke 12:32; cf. vv. 22-34 for context). That God's people bring him pleasure suggests that expanding the circle of his relationships, even at great cost, may be the best explanation for his choice to create.

Although it is not common to ask why God created, many want to know how God created. Two points must be kept in mind when considering this question: First, all truth is God's truth; he is the source of all truth. As we have seen, science is a human interpretation of the facts of God's creation and theology is a human interpretation of the facts of God's revelation in the Scriptures. Because God is truth (and, therefore, is perfectly consistent), right science and right theology never conflict. The world that science interprets is the world that God created. The Word that we study is the Word that God revealed. God does not lie; his world and his Word, rightly interpreted, do not conflict.

Second, we need to keep in mind that the Bible was not given to satisfy our curiosity but to teach us those things we need to know in order to live a life pleasing to God now and to prepare us to spend eternity with him in heaven. Since the question how God created is not essential to faith and life, we should not expect the Bible to answer that question. The Bible (and especially the first two chapters of Genesis) very clearly answers the question of origins—"God created"—but it is not intended to describe how God created. This seems clear from the fact that God gave us, in Genesis 1 and Genesis 2, two accounts of creation. In Genesis 1, the animals were created first and Adam and Eve were created last. In Genesis 2, Adam was created first, then the animals, and finally Eve. It seems as if God were cautioning us, "It's not about how or when; what you need to understand clearly is who."

Keeping these two facts in mind opens the opportunity for Christians to engage in and to embrace the highest levels of science. It is totally appropriate for us to pursue a deep understanding of this universe that God has made—the stellar universe, the ecological universe, and the nuclear universe! We also understand, however, that all naturalistic assumptions, hypotheses, and theories—i.e., all that begins by denying the supernatural and, thus, the existence and revelation of God—are inappropriate and must be rejected. They are dead ends from the outset.

We may never know how or when God created. As scientists generate possible explanations, we must be prepared to test them empirically, for consistency with God's world, and rationally, for consistency with our understanding of God's word. At points, we may conclude that we need to adjust our understanding of the Bible but we must be careful never to twist the Scriptures to fit our science. We are not surprised with the order we observe in the universe because our God is orderly. Isaiah wrote, "For thus says the LORD, who created the heavens (he is God!), who formed the earth and made it (he established it; he did not create it empty [or unformed, or chaotic], he formed it to be inhabited!): 'I am the LORD, and there is no other'" (Isaiah 45:18).

Wait a minute! If God loves us (as we know he does) and he created this world to be our special home, we might wonder why the world is so hostile and dangerous. In the last chapter we saw that sin is the root cause of our pain and the pain we cause to others. Nevertheless, there also are problems and pains that are not caused by humans. A tiger ravages a village in India. Shark attacks multiply up and down the coasts of the Carolinas and Australia. Floods sweep away tens of thousands of homes and hundreds of lives in Pakistan. An earthquake and tsunami devastate villages in Indonesia and thousands of miles away in Sri Lanka. Another earthquake triggers devastating landslides in Nepal or China. What's with this?

This is not what God intended and (thankfully!) things won't always be this way. When God created our first parents, he placed them in a perfect garden that was free from "the rule of fang and claw." At the end of this age, when God reigns over his people, furthermore, the Bible tells us, "The wolf shall dwell with the lamb, and the leopard shall lie down with the young goat, and the calf and the lion and the fattened calf together; and a little child shall lead them" (Isaiah 11:6; cf. Isaiah 65:25). The trauma and carnage that is so much a part of the world we know will be history. In God's future kingdom, things will be as he intends them.

In the meantime, however, we live with trauma and carnage. It's not fun! Why this mess?

When Adam and Eve sinned, they were driven out of that perfect garden. God was—and is—grieved by human sin but he was not surprised. He knew that humans—Adam and Eve and you and I—would choose to rebel against him and would go their own way. In anticipation of our rebellion, God provided a means of redemption and reconciliation. Jesus, the incarnate Second Person of the Trinity, is "the lamb of God who takes away the sin of the world!" (John 1:29).

In anticipation of our sinful rebellion, God also provided a world that is suited to—and that reflects—our fallenness. Our mess has become this world's mess. Our brokenness is reflected in the brokenness of this world in which we live. Fang and claw do reign. Earthquakes and hurricanes and floods and forest fires happen. They remind us that things are not as God intended, that a better place awaits us when we align ourselves with him. Furthermore, God often uses the dangers, the trauma, and the pain inflicted by this world to remind us of our dependence on himself.

Nevertheless, we must never forget that this is not what God intended. Paul employs the literary technique of personification to make this clear. He writes,

> For the creation waits with eager longing for the revealing of the sons of God. For the creation was subjected to futility, not willingly, but because of him who subjected it, in hope that the creation itself will be set free from its bondage to corruption and obtain the freedom of the glory of the children of God. For we know that the whole creation has been groaning together in the pains of childbirth until now. And not only the creation, but we ourselves, who have the firstfruits of the Spirit, groan inwardly as we wait eagerly for adoption as sons, the redemption of our bodies. (Romans 8:19-23)

When God's people receive their eternal bodies, freed from disease and decay, the whole creation also will be transformed, freed from tragedy and trauma, and become what God intended it to be—our perfect, eternal home.

For now, however, we live with tragedy and trauma, looking to God as our provider, protector, and our great physician. When we don't see him in our circumstances, we embrace him by faith, knowing that even in tragedy and trauma our circumstances are not out of his control. He loves us and he desires to use even very hard things to draw us into a closer relationship with himself. With this perspective, we recognize that the world God has provided for us truly is our special home.

**Let's Talk About It**

- How do you respond to the suggestion, when thinking about creation, that we focus on "not how or when, but who"?

- Was it merciful or mean for God to give us a world that now is filled with "tragedy and trauma"? Why is it merciful, or why is it mean?

# CHAPTER 11

## How Things Work

Have you noticed that life seems to include a generous portion of the unexpected—some delightful, some dismaying, and some just plain painful? How we respond to the unexpected relates directly to our understanding of how things work. Of course, there are things that simply work on physical laws. If you pick up a burning ember, you will get burned. If you choose an immoral lifestyle, your odds of contracting a sexually transmitted disease, of frying your brain, or of developing cirrhosis of the liver are much higher. We understand those things; it's the unexpected that gives us problems.

Some would have us believe that the universe and the circumstances of our lives are like a massive pinball machine, with individuals and events bouncing off one another in totally random patterns. The circumstances of your life are unpredictable because they largely are determined by chance. Your luck may be good on some days and bad on others but you learn to take the good with the bad. There is no accounting for luck.

Other people believe that the circumstances of our lives are controlled by fate. There are events that must occur and they shape our lives. Hindus call this "karma." They believe that our experiences in this life, whether good or bad, are determined by our behavior in previous lives. We have no control over karma, we only can accept it and respond to it in the best ways possible. Americans and Europeans who embrace "New Age Spirituality" also believe their lives are shaped by karma, or fate.

Two or three centuries ago Deism was a popular view that acknowledged God as creator of the universe but did not recognize his involvement in the world today. The God of Deism was a "clockmaker God"—he created the world as a complicated time piece, wound it up, and set it to run on its own. Because the world God created is ordered, choices and events have consequences but this should not be viewed as Divine intervention; it simply shows that that this universe works. If you obey the laws of the universe, things go well; if you don't, you will reap the consequences.[22]

When we look to the Bible to understand how things work, we find a very different picture. Both the course of human history and the circumstances of our individual lives are controlled by a loving and omnipotent, absolutely sovereign God. Nothing occurs that is beyond his control; he is able to bring good out of evil and to bring evil persons to justice.

When Joseph's brothers sold him into slavery it was hard to see how anything good could come of such a horrible act. Years later, however, Joseph was able to say, "You meant evil against me but God meant it for good, to bring it about that many people [i.e., Jacob's extended family, numbering seventy people] should be kept alive, as they are today" (Genesis 50:20). The evil choice of Joseph's brothers was known to God, so he arranged that the specific traders who bought Joseph would take him to Egypt where he would rise, through a series of divinely ordered circumstances, to a position of power. Thus, Joseph could rescue and provide for his family, including the brothers who had sold him.

We also clearly see God's involvement in human history in the biblical story of Daniel. Nebuchadnezzar, a Babylonian king under whom Daniel served, learned the hard way that God's "dominion is an everlasting dominion, and his kingdom endures from generation to generation, all the inhabitants of the earth are accounted as nothing, and he does according to his will among the host of heaven and among the inhabitants of the earth; and none can stay his hand or say to him, 'What have you done?'" (Daniel 4:34-35; for background, read all of Daniel 4). Daniel understood God's involvement in human history before Nebuchadnezzar figured it out. He said, "[God] changes times and seasons; he removes kings and sets up kings" (Daniel 2:21).

David also understood God's control of human history. Although "the kings of the earth set themselves and the rulers take counsel

---

[22] A fourth alternative to the biblical perspective is Spiritism, that the events of life are determined by good and evil spirits that actively shape the circumstances of our lives. We will discuss this perspective in the chapter on "Our Mortal Enemies."

together against the Lord and against his anointed," David notes, "He who sits in the heavens laughs; the Lord holds them in derision" (Psalm 2:2, 4). Another psalmist sang, "Surely the wrath of man shall praise you" (Psalm 76:10).

Pitcher pumps are rare these days but in Asia I've watched children filling buckets with water under a pitcher pump. As one child pumps, the other uses his hands to direct the water into one bucket after another. Solomon must have had a similar picture in mind when he wrote, "The king's heart is a stream of water in the hand of the LORD; he turns it wherever he will" (Proverbs 21:1).

Theologians refer to God's sovereign control of history and of the circumstances of our lives as "providence." The doctrine of God's providence raises an interesting question, however. Does God always get what he wants? If everything that occurs really is within his control, then it may seem reasonable to expect that God does get everything he wants.

The Bible makes clear, however, that God does not always get what he wants. After Adam and Eve sinned and were driven out of the garden, things went downhill quickly. We read, "The LORD saw that the wickedness of man was great in the earth, and that every intention of the thoughts of his heart was only evil continually, and the LORD was sorry that he had made man on the earth, and it grieved him to his heart" (Genesis 6:5-6). That "the LORD was sorry that he had made man" does not mean that God was surprised or had second thoughts about his decision to create; he knew when he created humans exactly what they would do. Nevertheless, watching human evil play out and seeing people hurt in the process (which inevitably happens) saddened him, "it grieved him to his heart." That was not what he wanted for that generation and it's not what he wants for our generation, either. Could he have prevented it? Yes, but not without violating his image in us that includes our capacity to make choices, including (often) bad choices.

We see a similar response from the heart of God to King Saul's progressive disobedience of the Lord's clear commands, delivered through the prophet, Samuel. In the end we read, "the LORD regretted that he had made Saul king over Israel" (1 Samuel 15:35; read the whole chapter for context). What's this! Didn't God know in advance how Saul's reign would end? Of course he did; God is omniscient. Nevertheless, the way Saul's reign ended didn't make God happy.

We see this again as God pleads with his people who felt they were rotting in Babylonian captivity, saying, "As I live, declares the Lord GOD, I have no pleasure in the death of the wicked, but that the wicked turn from his way and live; turn back, turn back from your evil ways, for why will you die, O house of Israel?" (Ezekiel 33:11; cf. verse 10 and 18:30-32). Israel did not turn back, however; God did not get what he wanted.

Jesus also grieved over the way the religious leaders and the people of Jerusalem rejected the grace God offered them through his calls to repent. Shortly before his death, Jesus agonized over Jerusalem, saying, "O Jerusalem, Jerusalem, the city that kills the prophets and stones those who are sent to it! How often would I have gathered your children together as a hen gathers her brood under her wings, and you would not!" (Matthew 23:37). Obviously, rejection by his own people is not what Jesus wanted but the choice was theirs, not his.

It still is true that God does not get what he wants. Peter, inspired by the Holy Spirit, tells us that God is "not wishing that any should perish, but that all should reach repentance" (2 Peter 3:9). Nevertheless, we know that many will perish; Jesus even told us that "the gate is wide and the way is easy that leads to destruction, and those who enter by it are many" (Matthew 7:13). How that must grieve God's heart.

Although God does not always get what he wants, his purposes are not frustrated. When Saul failed to lead Israel as God intended, God chose David to establish the kingdom. As we have seen, God "removes kings and sets up kings" and he controls the circumstances of our lives, as well. He will not force us to do what he wants but if we refuse to serve him, he will use someone else who is willing and we will be the losers. That's why, both on the global scale of world events and on the personal scale of the circumstances of my life, it is appropriate to recognize that history is his-story.

This truth is critical to understanding Paul's teaching about God's dealings with Israel, in Romans 9. In verses 10-16, Paul considers the case of Jacob and Esau. When God said, "Jacob I loved but Esau I hated" (verse 13) it sounds like God chose to "hate" and reject Esau without any reason, just arbitrarily. Furthermore, as Paul points out, that statement was made "though [the children] were not yet born and had done nothing either good or bad" (verse 11). So, did God just arbitrarily choose Jacob over Esau?

Paul seems to encourage this interpretation by quoting God's word to Moses, "I will have mercy on whom I have mercy, and I will have compassion on whom I have compassion" (Romans 9:15; cf. Exodus 33:19). That may sound like God asserts his right to be arbitrary. That can't be, however; it directly contradicts everything else God has revealed about himself. God loves justice (Psalm 33:5); he does not play favorites (Romans 2:11). When we are tempted to interpret a passage of Scripture in a way that contradicts other Scriptures, we should realize that we've got something wrong.

It is important to note that Paul's point in this passage is that God's choice is not based on our behavior. We cannot earn his favor; the critical issue is God's "call" (verse 11). If we go back to the Exodus passage, we can see that God is intentional, rather than arbitrary, in dispensing his grace. Moses asked to see God's glory (Exodus 33:18). God said that Moses had overreached, "for man shall not see me and live" (Exodus 33:20). God agreed that Moses should see the effects of his presence (which probably is the best interpretation of Exodus 33:23) but God's full glory is too much for any human in this life. Thus, the phrase Paul quoted originally affirmed God's intentionality in dispensing his favor rather than arbitrariness.

A better interpretation of Romans 9:10-16 recognizes that God's "hatred" of Esau and choice of Jacob was based on his foreknowledge of their individual (and free) responses to the grace extended to them. Esau did not value God's mercy toward him (represented by his birthright) and traded it for a bowl of stew (Genesis 25:29-34). Jacob valued God's blessings and accepted the mercy and grace God offered him (Genesis 28:10-22; 35:1-15). Paul's point is that Jacob and Esau were not accepted or rejected by God on the basis of what they did but, rather, on the basis of their response to his grace.

Someone might say, "Wait a minute. Isn't their response to grace a 'work'? Paul specifically says God's choice is not based on works." No, our response to God's grace is not attributable to any effort on our part; it is not something we do to earn merit. Our response to God's grace simply is the exercise of our capacity to choose, something that is essential to our creation in God's image. Choosing to receive the grace that God offers me does not earn merit; the grace is God's! On the other hand, choosing to reject God's grace inevitably leads to sin, which incurs my guilt. So when I appropriate God's grace, I do not earn merit—the glory belongs to him. When I reject God's grace, on the other hand, I can't blame the resulting sin on God—the guilt belongs to me.

Paul next introduces the illustration of Pharaoh (Romans 9:17-18), which he summarizes with the observation that God "has mercy on whomever he wills, and he hardens whomever he wills." Again, it may appear that Paul suggests that God is capricious, but we know that cannot be true. God is sovereign—he acts in keeping with his own character, his acts are not determined by anyone or anything outside himself—but he is not capricious.

A more consistent interpretation emerges from careful reflection on the case of Pharaoh. God desired to deliver his people from slavery in Egypt but he also wanted to display his power and make his name known throughout the earth (Exodus 9:16; cf. Exodus 7:5). To do that, God needed a Pharaoh on the throne of Egypt who would refuse to acknowledge that he is God or to release the Israelites to leave Egypt. There must have been many claimants to the throne of Egypt at that time but God ordered events so this particular Pharaoh would be the ruler of Egypt when Moses entered his court. God knew this Pharaoh would refuse to let the Israelites leave (Exodus 3:19), thus setting the stage for God's mighty demonstration of his greatness.

Romans 9:18 concludes with reference to God's "hardening" the heart of "whomever he wills." There are two aspects of this statement that require careful interpretation. First, what does it mean for God to "harden" a person's heart—in this case, Pharaoh's? Some understand "hardening" to mean that God causes people to sin. In fact, the New Living Translation even translates this phrase, "he makes some people refuse to listen." That flatly contradicts the clear fact that God loves all people, has provided for their redemption, and desires that all would come to repentance and fellowship with himself. God does not act contrary to his desires.

To understand God's "hardening" of Pharaoh (and of many people, since), we need to begin by acknowledging that all humans are sinners. That means our natural inclination, in every situation, is to sin—to rebel against God and to pursue our own distorted desires and self-interests. The only reason any of us is not much more evil than we are is because of God's grace. In grace, God extends to us the spiritual help we need to choose what is right, what is consistent with God's will and character. God does not force his grace upon us, however; he offers it and it is up to us to accept it and act on it.

Although God by nature is gracious, we must not presume on his grace. If we reject his grace repeatedly, he can withdraw his grace. When he does that, our sin nature takes over and things get worse and worse. This is what the Bible refers to as "hardening the heart." Initially, Pharaoh hardened his own heart (Exodus 7:13, 22; 8:15, 32), rejecting the grace that God offered him. Finally, however, God withdrew his grace, with the effect that Pharaoh's rebellious and sinful nature blinded him in his negativity (Exodus 9:12; 14:8). Although God is patient and loving, he is not obligated to extend grace to us. In Pharaoh's case, there came a point at which God withdrew his grace and Pharaoh's heart was "hardened."

The second thing to be understood is God's "willingness" to harden people's hearts. The rest of Scripture teaches that God is loving, he "desires all people to be saved and to come to the knowledge of the truth" (1 Timothy 2:4), so we can be sure that God does not desire to withdraw his grace from anyone. Nevertheless, there are those, like Pharaoh, who repeatedly and persistently reject God's offer of grace. There comes a point at which God "gives them up" to their own passions (cf. Romans 1:26, in context). God offers grace but he will not contend forever with those who are rebellious (Isaiah 57:16, in context).

Finally, Paul defends God's right to do what he chooses (Romans 9:19-24), i.e., to act in keeping with his own character. We have no right to criticize God. To make his point, Paul takes it to an extreme. Even if God were to create some for destruction and others for glory (which he did not), we would have no basis for complaint. God is sovereign; he can do as he wills. What he wills, however, is always to act in keeping with his character. God loves the world (John 3:16). God has provided redemption for all (1 John 2:2). God is not willing that any should perish (2 Peter 3:9). He has created all humans like himself so he can have intimate fellowship with us. We have sinned—corporately and individually—and we deserve damnation. If we refuse to accept the provision he has made for us, God has no option but to consign us to the consequences of our guilt. He always acts in keeping with his character; "He cannot deny himself" (2 Timothy 2:13; see verses 11-12 for context). Even those who suffer "destruction" have no right to criticize him.

This passage illustrates God's control of global history and of the circumstances of our lives. In the case of Jacob and Esau, in the case of Joseph and Pharaoh, and in the case of you and I, God is in complete control of the circumstances of our lives. God desires our good, he delights to give good gifts to his children (Matthew 7:11), and he orders our circumstances to lead us to himself. We can resist his grace—which clearly is dangerous—but God's purposes will not be frustrated; he will accomplish his purposes in other ways.

Recognizing that God's purposes will be accomplished is both a warning and a source of confidence for us. It is a warning not to resist God's grace and his purposes in our lives. We can, but if we do, we will suffer. He really does love us and his desires for us are best. It also is a source of confidence. As we embrace the grace that God extends to us, we can be confident that God's purposes will be accomplished in and through us. We have nothing to fear. He is loving and he is sovereign.

**Let's Talk About It**

- How does it make you feel to realize that God is in complete control of the circumstances of your life, that even when you (or others) mess up God can bring good out of the mess?

- It is sobering to realize that God has given me the capacity to refuse his grace—the spiritual help that I need in order to choose what is right and fair and kind and holy. It is even more sobering to realize that persistent rejection of God's grace can lead to his decision to withhold grace, thus confirming my choice of wickedness. What do you do with that? How does it make you want to respond to God's grace as you experience it?

# CHAPTER 12

## The Power of Prayer

Since we have a God who loves us, who is all powerful, and who controls the circumstances of our lives, it is reasonable for us to express to him our love, our thankfulness for his care and provision, and our requests.

Over and over again the Bible encourages prayer. Jesus, himself, was a man of prayer. He prayed on the occasion of his baptism by John (Luke 3:21). At the beginning of his public ministry he sought solitude in order to spend time in prayer (Mark 1:35). As news about his ministry began to spread, Jesus guarded times of solitude and prayer (Luke 5:15-16). He spent the night in prayer before appointing twelve as apostles (Luke 6:12-13). After teaching and feeding a crowd of 5,000, he retreated to a mountain and spent an evening in prayer (Matthew 14:23). Before revealing his impending death to the twelve, Jesus "was praying alone" (Luke 9:18-22). Jesus' glory was revealed to Peter, James, and John on an occasion that began as a prayer retreat (Luke 9:28-29). Lazarus had been dead for four days but he walked out of his tomb after Jesus prayed (John 11:38-44). He prayed fervently on the night before his crucifixion (Luke 22:41-44). It was the prayer life of Jesus that moved the Twelve to ask him to teach them to pray (Luke 11:1-4). Since prayer was so much a part of Jesus' life, ought it not be even more a part of ours?

Jesus had much to say about the importance of prayer. He urged his followers "always to pray and not lose heart" (Luke 18:1). He taught that there are spiritual battles that can be won only through prayer (Mark 9:25-29). He told us that God is like a father who delights to give good gifts to his children (Matthew 7:9-11) and he assures us that believing prayer will be answered (Mark 11:24). He also assured his disciples (and us) that he would do whatever is asked in his name, "that the Father may be glorified in the Son" (John 14:13-14). "Until now," he said, "you have asked nothing in my name. Ask, and you will receive, that your joy may be full" (John 16:24). Paul points out that the alternative to anxiety is prayer and urges his readers, in every situation, to "let your requests be made known to God" (Philippians 4:6).

It often is said that God has three answers to prayer, "Yes," "No," and "Wait." Those who say this typically point to Jesus' unanswered prayer in Gethsemane to "let this cup[23] pass from me" (Matthew 26:39) and to Paul's unanswered prayer for deliverance from his "thorn in the flesh" (2 Corinthians 12:7-8). These should not cause us to doubt God's promises to give what we ask in prayer, however, since in each of these cases God revealed that the request would not be granted. In the case of Jesus' prayer for deliverance from the cup of his suffering, Jesus conditioned his request by expressing his acceptance of the Father's will (Matthew 26:42) and Luke tells us that "there appeared to him an angel from heaven, strengthening him" (Luke 22:43). In Paul's case, God specifically responded, "My grace is sufficient for you, for my power is made perfect [or is perfectly displayed] in [your] weakness" (2 Corinthians 12:7-9). In light of the many promises that our prayers will be answered, therefore, it seems appropriate for us to pray, expecting that God will do as we ask, unless we receive specific guidance to the contrary.

Rather than saying that "God has three answers to prayer," it is more helpful to examine our practice of prayer. The Scriptures indicate that unanswered prayer more likely is due to our failure to pray properly rather than to God's unwillingness to do what we ask. The Psalmist reminds us that unconfessed sin prevents God from hearing our prayers (Psalm 66:18; cf. Isaiah 1:15; James 4:3). Closely related is any unwillingness on our part to forgive others who hurt or offend us; that, too, prevents God from granting our requests (Matthew 6:14-15).

Jesus repeatedly taught that prayer should be made "in my name" (John 15:16; cf. John 15:7, 1 John 3:22). That does not mean only that

---

[23] "This cup" usually is understood to refer to his impending scourging, trial, and crucifixion, and thus as a prayer that was unanswered. Buswell argues, however, that "the 'cup' from which Jesus asked to be delivered in Gethsemane was physical collapse and death in the garden before He reached the cross" (J.O. Buswell, Jr. *A Systematic Theology of the Christian Religion*, Vol 2, Grand Rapids: Zondervan, 1963, p 62). If Buswell is right, this prayer of Jesus was answered as an angel "strengthened him" (Luke 22:43-44).

we are to add "...in the name of Jesus..." to the end of our prayers. In Hebrew culture, a person's name represented his character. By instructing us to pray "in my name," Jesus invited us to expect our prayers to be answered when our lives are aligned with his and warned that a life that is not aligned with his cannot expect answered prayers. Of course, God sometimes does answer the prayers of sinners but that is evidence of his mercy. The person who is living outside of God's will cannot expect her or his prayers to be answered.

On at least two occasions, Jesus also warned against giving up when answers to our prayers are delayed, pointing to lack of persistence as a cause of unanswered prayers (Luke 11:5-10; 18:1-8). God wants his children to believe that he will give them what they ask (Mark 11:24; cf. Matthew 21:22). Lack of faith—unbelief that God will, in fact, answer our prayers—actually inhibits God from doing what we have asked. That is why the teaching that God sometimes answers "Yes" and sometimes "No" is so insidious; it undermines our faith in answered prayer. If our hearts are open before God, if we have confessed our sins and have forgiven others who have sinned against us, if our lives are honoring to Christ, lived "in his name," and if we pray persistently, believing that God will do as we ask, we can be confident that God will honor his promises to give us what we have asked.

If we are tempted to doubt the power of prayer, we need only to look again at the Scriptures. James assures us that "The prayer of a righteous person has great power as it is working" (James 5:16). He then goes on to cite the account of Elijah's prayer, in response to which God withheld rain for three years and six months, then sent rain again when Elijah prayed (James 5:17-18). In response to Joshua's prayer, daylight was extended as Israel pursued the fleeing Amorites (Joshua 10:12-14). In response to prayer, God caused dew to collect only on the fleece Gideon laid and then only on the ground and not on the fleece (Judges 6:36-40). In response to Hannah's prayer, God gave a son to a woman who had been unable to conceive (1 Samuel 1:12-20). In response to Elijah's prayer, fire fell from heaven (i.e., lightning struck), vaporizing Elijah's sacrifice, the altar on which his sacrifice was laid, and water in the trench around the altar (1 Kings 18:36-38). In response to Hezekiah's prayer, Jerusalem was rescued from an overwhelming army that laid siege on the city (2 Kings 19: 14-20, 32-37). In response to Peter's prayer, a dead woman was restored to life (Acts 9:36-41). In response to the prayers of Christians, chains that bound Peter to his guards fell off, sentries were blinded, prison doors were opened, and Peter walked out to freedom (Acts 12:5-11).

In the face of such reports and the example and encouragement of our Lord, how can we doubt God's willingness to answer our prayers? Writing to the Corinthian Christians, Paul reminded them that "the weapons of our warfare are not of the flesh but have divine power to destroy strongholds" (2 Corinthians 10:4). Surely, prayer is our ultimate spiritual weapon.

## Let's Talk About It

- Think of a prayer of yours that has been unanswered. As you review the reasons suggested in this chapter, can you see reasons God may have chosen not (yet) to have answered this prayer?

- I have asked, "Since prayer was so much a part of Jesus' life, ought it not be even more a part of ours?" How do you respond to that? Do you need to take any steps to give prayer its appropriate priority in your life?

# CHAPTER 13

## God's Special Emissaries

Do you believe in angels?

The way you answer that question speaks volumes about your understanding of the nature of the universe. The Bible portrays a universe in which the physical world and the spiritual world are equally real and in which the two are intertwined.

That's not the operational perspective of most people in Western nations today. It is common, even for those who say they believe in angels, to assume that the events of life can be explained completely in terms of natural causes. It is the rare Western person who would assume that an unexpected event, whether good or bad, might be the result of divine, angelic, or demonic intervention, rather than by natural causes, whether ordered or random.

That is not the case, however, in much of the rest of the world; people in other cultures often have a keener perception of the physical-spiritual nature of the universe in which we live. As Westerners we find it easy to dismiss such views as superstitions or primitive folklore. If they were more scientifically informed, we assume, they would know better.

When we look to the Scriptures, we find a universe in which God is active and in which the natural order is a battleground between God and Satan, with angels and demons as spiritual combatants and with the lives of humans as the location of this struggle. This battle already has been won through the death of Christ (Colossians 2:15) but Satan and his forces continue to contest God's redemptive plan and to turn men and women away from the grace that God extends (Ephesians 6:11-12). We are not alone on this battlefield, however; God not only has given us his word and his Spirit, there are times when he sends angels to intervene on our behalf as well.

The word "angel" (*angelos*, ἄγγελος), which occurs 185 times in the New Testament, is best translated "messenger." Sometimes it is used in this sense of people (e.g., Matthew 11:10; Luke 7:24; James 2:25) but by far most of the uses clearly refer to supernatural, personal beings. The Bible indicates there are millions of them (Revelation 9:16; "twice ten thousand times ten thousand," if taken literally, equals 200 million; cf. Daniel 7:10).

One of the ways these supernatural beings serve God is by delivering messages to his people. The law was delivered to Moses by angels (Acts 7:53; cf. Galatians 3:19 and Hebrews 2:2) and an angel announced to the wife of Manoah that she would bear a son (Judges 13:3-7). When Daniel did not understand the vision he had been given by God, an angel was sent to reveal the meaning of the vision (Daniel 8:15-16). Prior to the birth of Jesus, angels appeared, first to Zechariah (Luke 1:11-20) and then to Mary (Luke 1:26-38) to announce the births of John ("the Baptist") and of the Messiah. Furthermore, when God chose "to show to his servants the things that must soon take place, he made it known by sending his angel to his servant John [the Apostle]" (Revelation 1:1).

Angels don't only deliver messages, however, they also guide and guard God's people. When Abraham sent his servant to get a wife for Isaac, his servant hesitated but Abraham assured him, "[God] will send his angel before you" (Genesis 24:7). God said he would send an angel to guard Israel as his people traveled through the desert on their way to the Promised Land (Exodus 23:20). Philip received directions from an angel when he was sent to bring news about Jesus to an Ethiopian official (Acts 8:26) and Cornelius was told by an angel where he would find Peter (Acts 10:3-7).

In addition to delivering messages and guiding and guarding God's people, God sometimes sends angels to protect his people and to deliver them from danger. When God was ready to destroy Sodom, he sent two angels to evacuate Lot and his family from that sinful city (Genesis 19:15-17). After spending a sleepless night while Daniel was in a den of lions, King Darius asked, "...has your God, whom you serve continually, been able to deliver you from the lions?" Imagine his amazement and relief when Daniel responded, "My God sent his angel and shut the lions' mouths and they have not harmed me" (Daniel 6:21-22). When the high priest and the Sadducees put the apostles in prison, and later, when Herod imprisoned Peter, the Lord sent an angel to release them (Acts 5:19-20; 12:7-10). Every deliverance may not be as dramatic as these but it should not surprise us that God sends his angels to deliver his people who are in distress, since he has promised this for those who fear him (Psalm 34:7; cf. Psalm 91:11-12).

The Bible also recounts occasions when angels provided tangible help when it was needed. When Sarah sent Hagar and her son away, Abraham gave her provisions that included only one container of water. When that ran out, Hagar and the boy seemed certain to die in the heat of the desert. As she was ready to give up, an angel appeared who encouraged her and pointed her to a well where water was available (Genesis 21:15-19). When Elijah had collapsed from hunger and exhaustion as he fled from Jezebel, an angel provided food for him (1 Kings 19:5-8). After Jesus had fasted for forty days and had been tempted by Satan, "angels came and ministered to him" (Matthew 4:11). Perhaps they brought him food as they had done for Elijah. "An angel from heaven" also appeared to strengthen Jesus as he agonized in prayer prior to his crucifixion (Luke 22:43). We are not told how Jesus was strengthened, but that certainly was a moment of great need and God the Father met the need of his Son at that moment through the ministry of an angel.

Should we expect angels to intervene in our lives today? There should be no question that God can send angels to minister to his people today, just as he did in biblical times. At the same time, as Jesus pointed out to Satan, we must never presume on God's provision (Matthew 4:5-7). There are numerous, credible reports, however, of ministries of encouragement, guidance, and deliverance by unknown persons who very well may be angels sent by God to help his people. Here is just one example.

In the late 1960s, when most highways in the Philippines were just two-lane roads, a van full of missionary women left the rural town where most were studying the Philippine language and culture to make the two-hour trip to Manila. Their mission agency had scheduled a women's retreat they were to attend. As they drove, they descended a long hill and rounded a corner into a populated area just as a man started across the road in front of them. When he looked up and saw the van approaching, he began to run, then panicked, reversed directions, and ran right in front of the van. There was nothing the driver could do; she hit the man and later learned that he had quickly died from his injuries.

In their course on Philippine culture, the women had been warned not to stop in such situations because of the danger of "instant justice." Nevertheless, dazed by the tragic and unexpected event, the driver stopped and the women began getting out of the van. Immediately, a vigilante crowd began to form. As the young missionary women were milling about, a VW Beetle pulled up and a well-dressed Filipino man got out. In English, he inquired who was the driver and instructed her to have her passengers get back in the van and follow him. The man in the VW Beetle led the van through a maze of one-way streets to the local police department where he took the driver and the passenger from the front seat to the desk sergeant. "These women have an incident to report," he said. As the women gave their identification and accident report to the desk sergeant, they turned to thank the man who had rescued them, only to find he had returned to his car and gone on his way.

Over the next several weeks, every attempt to trace the driver of that VW Beetle proved futile. There is little doubt that the situation from which he rescued the women quickly could have turned even more tragic had the women stayed on the scene. Nevertheless, the response of the man in the VW Beetle was entirely contrary to Filipino culture. To render assistance, in Philippine context, incurs inescapable personal obligation. Filipinos are loving and compassionate people but to avoid imposing obligation on others, they typically wait until assistance is requested before rendering it. Thus, for this man to stop, as he did, was very counter-cultural.

Who was this unknown man? Was he an angel, sent by God, to rescue a group of young missionary women who were in a very dangerous situation of which they were unaware? It is impossible to say. Nevertheless, if God were to send an angel into that situation, it seems probable the angel would have appeared as a well-dressed Filipino man in a VW Beetle.

Such stories should not amaze us. The Bible has so much to say about the ministry of angels to God's people. It tells us his angels are "ministering spirits, sent out to serve for the sake of those who are to inherit salvation" (Hebrews 1:13-14). Furthermore, we are urged "to show hospitality to strangers, for thereby some have entertained angels unawares" (Hebrews 13:2).

As Christians, we cannot afford to live in a one-dimensional universe. God intends us to understand that he actively intervenes in our lives, even through the ministry of angels. Without going to the excess of seeing an angel behind every bush, we should be alert to the tangible ways God works to guide and guard us. Sometimes that may include sending an angel to provide exactly what we need.

**Let's Talk About It**

- To what extent are you aware of the physical-spiritual nature of the universe in which you live? Why do you suppose Satan is so eager to encourage us to focus on the physical?

- Have you heard other stories of Christians who encountered individuals who rendered needed help or guidance but who later were untraceable? How should we strike a balance between credulity and healthy skepticism with respect to such stories?

# CHAPTER 14

## Our Mortal Enemies

One of the most difficult questions a person can ask is, "Why is there so much evil in the world?" Philosophers have struggled to answer the question of "the origin of evil" for at least 2,500 years. The Bible provides important clues but it does not give a final answer to that question. Here's an important principle to keep in mind:

> The Bible was not given to satisfy our curiosity but to teach us those things we need to know to live a life that is pleasing to God now and to prepare us to spend eternity with him in heaven.

When the Bible doesn't provide a clear answer to a theological question, therefore, we should accept the fact that we really don't need to know the answer. With respect to the problem of evil, what we need to know—what God has revealed in the Bible—is that each of us is egocentric to the core and (as we saw in Chapter 9) that makes big trouble. When God created the first man and woman, he placed them in a perfect environment—a "garden"—but soon evil entered the picture and things have been hard ever since. Where did that "evil" come from?

The Bible tells us that evil existed before our first parents sinned but it does not tell us much about the origin of evil. In the Genesis narrative, it was "the serpent" that tempted Adam and Eve (Genesis 3:1-6). The word that is used is the common word for "snake" but we need not jump to the conclusion that there was a talking reptile in the garden with Adam and Eve. The New Testament speaks of a person who is "the deceiver of the whole world" and refers to him as "that ancient serpent" (Revelation 12:9).

In the last chapter we saw that angels serve God and his people. As personal beings, angels—like humans—have the capacity to make choices. The Bible indicates that there was a time long ago when some of the angels rebelled against God (cf. Jude 6 and 2 Peter 2:4). Although humans currently have the opportunity to be reconciled to God, the Bible clearly teaches that will not always be the case (Matthew 25:46; see verses 31-46 for context). It would appear that the moral condition of angels—both those that serve God and those in rebellion against him—already is fixed.

The fallen angels, or demons, have as their leader one who most often is referred to in the Bible as Satan (Job 1:6; Mark 1:13; Acts 5:3). Some see the figurative language used to prophesy the demise of the kings of Babylon (Isaiah 14:12-15) and Tyre (Ezekiel 28:12-19) as oblique descriptions of Satan's fall, but there is nothing explicit in the text or context to support this interpretation. By studying the clear teaching of the Bible about the character and activities of Satan, however, we can learn much about his associates and underlings, as well.

We already know that Biblical names often are significant in revealing character. The name, "Satan," means "enemy" or "adversary." The generic term applied to this "ancient serpent" is "the devil" (Matthew 4:1; James 4:7) and is derived from the term "slanderer." As John described the visions recorded in the book of Revelation, he used the names "Abaddon" (Hebrew) and "Apollyon" (Greek), both of which mean "destroyer" (Revelation 9:11). Paul refers to him as "Belial" (2 Corinthians 6:15), which means "death."

Other names used for Satan in the scriptures reveal the position which he holds. He is "the prince of demons" (Matthew 9:34), "the angel [or messenger] of the bottomless pit" (Revelation 9:11), "the prince of the power of the air" (Ephesians 2:2), and "the god of this world" (2 Corinthians 4:4). These names reflect Satan's role as leader of the demonic forces and of the system of world cultures and structures that are opposed to God.

In other passages, we find descriptions of specific activities that are characteristic of Satan. Jesus described him as "a murderer from the beginning" and said he "has nothing to do with the truth, because there is no truth in him. When he lies, he speaks out of his own character [or, he speaks his native language], for he is a liar and the father of lies" (John 8:44). Jesus also engaged Satan as "tempter" (Matthew 4:3), and identified him as "the enemy" (Matthew 13:39). Paul urged Christians to be done with the Godless lifestyle of the past in which they followed "the spirit that is now at work in the sons of disobedience" (Ephesians 2:2). Peter recognized him as "the adversary" (1 Peter 5:8). John recorded a vision in which "the accuser of our brothers [i.e., of fellow Christians] ... who accuses them day and night before God" was thrown out of heaven (Revelation 12:10).

From the various names applied to Satan in the Scriptures and from the activities attributed to him, we get the picture that this is one bad character! He is our mortal enemy, bent on misleading, slandering, and finally destroying us. He is absolutely unprincipled in his pursuit of our destruction (1 Peter 5:8; cf. 2 Corinthians 2:11). Furthermore, he is very powerful and he leads an army of demons who are aligned with his mission to lead us into sin and to recruit us to his destructive cause. Ultimately, however, Satan is God's enemy, determined, by capturing humans (cf. 2 Timothy 2:26), to frustrate God's desire to redeem a people who will share his character and his relational intimacy.

In most of the world—all but the West[24]—the dominant worldview is animism. From region to region, the major world religions— Christianity, Islam, Buddhism, Hinduism, and others—are shaped by and, in various ways, accommodated to animism. (This is a great challenge to Biblical Christianity.) Although expressions of animism differ, generally it includes recognition of a benevolent, monotheistic God who is remote from the lives of humans. Of greater immediate concern among animists is the spirit world that shapes our circumstances from day to day. While some spirits are good, many are evil and are intent on harming us. Obtaining ways to protect oneself from these spirits who bring tragedy, illness, suffering, and death, therefore, is a daily concern. This is done by offering gifts to placate the spirits, by obtaining amulets or potions to protect oneself from their powers, by communicating with spirits through mediums, and by seeking the assistance of shamans— religious specialists who exercise power in the spirit world. It also is possible, however, to engage the spirits through hexes and spells to curse and harm one's enemies. Ultimately, animism is about gaining power in the spirit world for one's protection and for bringing evil on one's enemies.

---

[24] In the Western world—Western Europe, North America, Australia, New Zealand— the dominant worldview is naturalism. One of the effects of globalization is the spread of naturalism to the non-Western world.

The culture in Ur, from which Abraham was called, and the cultures of the Promised Land, which God gave to his people, were animistic. The Bible provides very clear instructions on how we are to relate to demons: We are to have nothing to do with them. As the people of Israel camped on the border of the Promised Land, God spoke through Moses to warn about demonic practices of the inhabitants of the land they were soon to possess—practices that included child sacrifice, "divination" (i.e., using objects, like a Ouija board, to contact the spirits), fortune telling, interpretation of omens, sorcery, spirit mediums, wizardry (i.e., casting spells), and "necromancy," or communication with the dead (Deuteronomy 18:10-11). God, through Moses, explicitly states "whoever does these things is an abomination to the Lord" (Deuteronomy 18:12).

God hates all occult practices and commands his people to have nothing to do with them. This is not an unreasonable restriction, as we recognize by understanding Satan's intent; he wants to use fascination with and involvement in the occult—which really is demonic—to destroy us.

Paul tells us, too, that those who worship idols are worshiping demons (1 Corinthians 10:20). The idols worshipped by 21st Century citizens of Western nations tend to be economic and cultural, rather than objects carved from wood or stone, but the power they hold is no less demonic.

To blind us to God's revealed truth (cf. 2 Corinthians 4:3-4), Satan may appear as "an angel of light" (2 Corinthians 11:14). The secular mindset and every non-Christian religion is a stratagem of Satan to lead us to reject God's revealed truth. When we consider the supernatural power and destructive intent of Satan and the demons, we appreciate God's warning to avoid completely all contact with them.

When people understand the evil power and intent of Satan and the demons, it is natural to respond with fear. That, however, plays right into Satan's hand. God does not intend his people to live in fear. Fear is an instrument of Satan to intimidate and immobilize us. We need to recognize that Satan and the demons are defeated enemies. On the cross, God "disarmed the rulers and authorities [i.e., Satan and the demons] and put them to open shame by triumphing over them in [Jesus]" (Colossians 2:15).

Paul wrote those words as he was under house arrest in Rome (see Acts 28:16, 30-31). This was a period of expansion of the Roman Empire. As victorious generals returned from the battle front to the capitol city, they marched into the city, followed by their troops, and behind them, in chains, were hundreds of captives they had taken, as proof of their victory. No doubt Paul had witnessed several such victory processions during his time of imprisonment. This is the image he employs in Colossians 2 to describe Jesus' triumph over Satan and the demons. They are defeated enemies, put on public display as trophies of his victory over the powers of sin and death.

John also employs a warfare metaphor as he describes a spiritual battle that results in Satan and the demons being thrown out of heaven. The instrument of their defeat, John tells us, was "the blood of the Lamb" (Revelation 12:11; see verses 7-12 for context). Jesus' redeeming death on the cross won victory over Satan and the demons so that they no longer have power over us. As we accept the salvation Christ offers, we participate in that victory.

Occasionally, in the American church, there is a flurry of interest in spiritual warfare and the demonic. This is a tactic of Satan to distract the church from its missional task of disciple-making and prophetic engagement with sin and injustice in society. In truth, the American church has almost no experience with demonic powers. This is because Satan's purposes are best served, given America's naturalistic worldview, by avoiding displays of power and by suggesting that reports of the demonic are superstitions held only by the unsophisticated. (This could change, however, with the arrival of those whose worldview is not Christian or if fascination with the "paranormal," the occult, and Wicca were to grow.) In contrast, the global Church and those in non-Western societies know all too well the power of the demonic. Christians pose as experts on the demonic and on spiritual warfare only at great risk to themselves and to Gospel witness.

It is vitally important for Christians to avoid all contact with the occult. We never should look for an opportunity to confront demons. If God brings us into a situation where demonic encounter is unavoidable, however, we need not be fearful. Our mortal enemy already has been defeated; what we see now are just his death spasms. When he attempts to assert authority or control, we can expose him as the liar he is, we can remind him that he already has been defeated by Jesus on the cross, and we can command him, in the name of Jesus, to leave us alone. Only Jesus reigns!

**Let's Talk About It**

- What strikes you as you reflect on the names assigned to Satan in the Scriptures?

- Since we know that Satan's purpose is to destroy us, why are we so fascinated with learning more about the occult? What does that tell us about ourselves and our culture? What does it tell us about Satan's tactics?

# CHAPTER 15

## The Man Like Us

Christians look to Jesus as "the founder and perfecter of our faith" (Hebrews 12:2) but who is he? Does it really matter whether he is God, or human? Is it even possible that he could be both God and human, as we have heard? Isn't that self-contradictory?

Jesus' contemporaries stumbled on these questions (John 5:18), so it should not surprise us that they persist today. Most people realize that Jesus is a man who lived 2000 years ago. In fact, most people agree that he was a very great man—perhaps even the greatest man who ever lived—but many would like to stop there. They are uncomfortable with the fact that Jesus' followers recognize him as God.

Paul wrote the Epistle to the Colossians to refute a heresy which denied that Jesus is God. Following his greeting and a prayer for Christians in Colossae, he states his thesis succinctly: "He [i.e., Jesus] is the image of the invisible God, the firstborn of all creation" (Colossians 1:15). Paul (moved by the Holy Spirit) affirms that the man, Jesus, accurately represents the eternal God. Both his character and capacities are divine. By adding that Jesus is "the firstborn of all creation," Paul asserts Jesus' priority over everything else that exists. Phillips captures Paul's meaning when he translates, "Now Christ is the visible expression of the invisible God. He existed before creation began."[25]

As Paul explores the implications of Jesus' deity, he argues, it is neither appropriate nor necessary for Christians to be misled by demonically inspired worldviews. "For in him the whole fullness of deity dwells bodily, and you have been filled in him, who is the head

---

[25] J.B. Phillips, *The New Testament in Modern English*, London: Geoffrey Bles, 1960.

of all rule and authority" (Col 2:9-10). "Rule and authority," as we saw in the last chapter, refers to demons. Their deceitful claims are not to be compared to the truth of the risen Christ who indwells Christians, Paul asserts, since he is 100% God.

Paul was not the only one to recognize that Jesus is God. John assures us that "the Word," Jesus whom John knew personally (John 1:14), "was God" (John 1:1). Speaking to a Roman military commander, Peter explained that Jesus "is Lord of all" (Acts 10:36)—a statement every Jew would recognize as affirming Jesus' deity. 1st Century Jews knew that to ascribe deity to anyone other than the God of the Bible is blasphemy of the highest order, yet confronted by the risen Jesus, Thomas exclaimed, "My Lord and my God!" (John 20:28).

The writer of the letter to Hebrew Christians also begins with a strong affirmation of Jesus' deity.

> Long ago, at many times and in many ways, God spoke to our fathers by the prophets, but in these last days he has spoken to us by his Son, whom he appointed the heir of all things, through whom also he created the world. He is the radiance of the glory of God and the exact imprint of his nature, and he upholds the universe by the word of his power. (Hebrews 1:1-3)

Jesus is the final revelation of God because he is God. If we want to know what God is like, the writer of Hebrews tells us, look at Jesus.

Of course, it is possible that all of Jesus' followers were mistaken about who he was. Some have insisted that Jesus himself never claimed to be God; he only referred to himself as the "son of man" (an affirmation of his humanity) and to God as his father. That suggestion may seem reasonable because we are separated by centuries, culture, and language from Jesus' use of that expression. To refer to God as his father, however, would not have been ambiguous to Jesus' contemporaries. They knew what he meant. They knew that Jesus was claiming to be "equal to God" (John 5:18). A "son" shares the DNA of his father. When Jesus claimed God as his father, his contemporaries heard this as a claim to be divine. John explains this is the reason the Jewish religious leaders plotted to kill him (cf. John 10:30-33).

Jesus' clearest declaration of his deity, however, is seen in his trial during the night before he was crucified. Under Jewish law, the High Priest had no right to ask Jesus to testify against himself, yet not only did he do so, he also placed Jesus under oath (Mark 14:60-61). Asked if he was the Messiah, the Son of God, Jesus responded, "I am" (Mark 14:62). For the Jewish leaders, that was the last straw. As a result, blasphemy—claiming to be God—was the charge on which he was found guilty (Mark 14:63-64).

Clearly, both Jesus and his disciples understood that he is God and his enemies understood that he claimed to be God, but there was no denying the fact that he was a man. He was a human who was born in Bethlehem, who grew up in Nazareth, and who lived and did much good in Galilee, taught throughout 1st Century Palestine, and died outside of Jerusalem. None of his contemporaries—neither his town mates (Mark 6:1-3) nor his enemies (John 10:33)—questioned that he was human.

Many people struggle to comprehend how one person could be both human and divine. As Christians in the past have affirmed this teaching of Scripture, they have stated that Jesus was one person with two natures. These terms, "person" and "nature," need to be defined.

You may recall that in Chapter 4 we defined "person" as a unique "self-center" with his or her (gender is irrelevant) own intellect, will, emotions, and capacity for personal relationships (e.g., communicating, loving, and covenanting). "Nature" simply refers to an essential set of attributes. We recognize a particular fruit as an "apple" because of the set of qualities, or attributes—size, shape, color, texture, structure, etc.—that are characteristic of that kind of fruit. Likewise, it is a unique set of attributes that characterize God—his eternality, omniscience, omnipotence, omnipresence, holiness, justice, love, etc. There also is a set of attributes that characterize humans; human attributes are similar to divine attributes, although human attributes are limited (whereas God's are unlimited) and imperfect (whereas God's are perfect). This should not be surprising, since God chose to create humans "in his image" (Genesis 1:26). If we line up divine and human attributes, they look like this:

| Divine Attributes | Human Attributes |
|---|---|
| Real | Real |
| Personal | Personal |
| Perfectly holy | Able to be holy |
| Perfectly just | Able to be just |
| Perfectly loving | Able to be loving |
| Perfectly faithful | Able to be faithful |
| Infinitely powerful | Limited in power |
| Infinitely present | Limited presence |
| Infinite in knowledge | Limited in knowledge |
| Infinite in time – Eternal | Limited in time – Immortal |

Humans are not naturally holy, just, loving, or faithful, but with the help of God's grace we can be. What we see is that for God to become human it is not necessary for him to divest himself of his divine attributes (i.e., to give up being God) but only to limit his use of his divine attributes so he would experience life as we do. This he did. The Bible teaches that Jesus, the Second Person of the Trinity, became human. The theological term for this is "incarnation"—literally, taking on flesh.

Paul describes in dramatic language what this meant for Jesus and the example of humility he set for us.

> Have this mind among yourselves, which is yours in Christ Jesus, who, though he was in the form of God, did not count equality with God a thing to be grasped, but made himself nothing, taking the form of a servant, being born in the likeness of men. And being found in human form, he humbled himself by becoming obedient to the point of death, even death on a cross. (Philippians 2:5-8)

To be "in the form of God" means to be God, to possess all of the divine attributes. The word translated "made himself nothing" is a form of the word *kenoo* (κενόω), which means "to empty" or "to render of no effect." It is the word from which theologians get the term "kenosis." When theologians speak of Jesus' "kenosis," they affirm Paul's teaching that the Second Person of the divine Trinity did not cling to his divine prerogatives (i.e., the independent use of his divine attributes) but "emptied himself" to become a servant, was born as a human, and died as a human—indeed, accepting the horrible death of crucifixion.

It is difficult for us to grasp the significance of this truth that God, in Christ, really accepted our limitations and faced life as we do. Indeed, many deny this truth by teaching that Jesus employed his divine attributes during his lifetime. Specifically, they point to the miracles done by Jesus to prove that he used his divine attributes. If Jesus used his divine attributes, however, then he did not face life as I do. When I get in trouble, I can't access divine attributes to extricate myself. In that case, Jesus' life loses much of its significance as an example for me.

It is very instructive to study the life of Jesus to see how he dealt with problems and temptations and to see how he explained the miracles he performed. When asked by his disciples when the end of the age would occur, Jesus said he did not know (Matthew 24:36). Was he lying? That cannot be! As God, of course, he was omniscient, but as part of "emptying himself" in order to face life as we do, he opted to limit access to his omniscience; he chose not to know that. Mark tells us that Jesus expressed amazement at the unbelief of his neighbors in Nazareth (Mark 6:6). Luke reports that the child Jesus learned like other children in his village; he "grew and became strong, filled with wisdom" (Luke 2:40). The writer of Hebrews also tells us, "Although he was a son, he learned obedience through what he suffered" (Hebrews 5:8). None of this suggests that Jesus employed his divine attribute of omniscience.

Wait, someone may say, don't the Gospels repeatedly report that Jesus knew what people were thinking (e.g., Matthew 9:2-4)? Doesn't that prove that he had access to his omniscience during his earthly life? Well, no. At least, that is not a necessary conclusion. John tells us that Jesus did not entrust himself to those who followed him "because he knew all people and needed no one to bear witness about man, for he himself knew what was in man" (John 2:24-25). He knew, better than any, the deceitfulness of the human heart (cf. Jeremiah 17:9). On many occasions when the gospel writers report that Jesus knew the thoughts of those in the crowds (e.g., Luke 6:8) there is no reason to assume Jesus' perception was different from ours when we say, "I know what you're thinking." Our nonverbal cues often betray our thoughts.

In ancient times, the king of Syria repeatedly was frustrated in his battle plans against Israel because God revealed to the prophet

Elisha what the king of Syria planned to do and Elisha conveyed that information to the king of Israel (see 2 Kings 6:8-12). As we will see in our next chapter, Jesus was a prophet. It is possible there also were occasions when God revealed to him the thoughts of others.

When Jesus was tempted by Satan, he did not employ his divine powers to banish Satan; he responded to Satan by quoting Scripture (Matthew 4:4, 7, 10). When challenged about the power he exercised over evil spirits, Jesus said his exorcisms were by the power of the Holy Spirit (Matthew 12:24-28). When the disciples inquired about their inability to cast out an evil spirit, Jesus did not respond by reminding them that they lacked divine attributes. Rather, he said "This kind cannot be driven out by anything but prayer" (Mark 9:28-29). When the disciples marveled at the wind and seas' response to Jesus' command, he did not say, "It's easy if you're omnipotent." Instead, he said, "Why are you so afraid? Have you still no faith?" (Mark 4:40). When Peter expressed amazement that a tree cursed by Jesus just a day earlier already was withered to the root, Jesus attributed this miracle to prayer and faith (Mark 11:20-24).

Prayer, faith, the power of the Holy Spirit—these all are available to every Christian. This helps us understand how Jesus could assure us, before leaving to return to heaven, that believers "will also do the works that I do; and greater works than these will [they] do, because I am going to the Father" (John 14:12). Jesus really did face life as we do.

That Jesus really was a person like us, that he truly faced life as we do, is not just a bit of Bible trivia; it is critical to our salvation. The writer of Hebrews makes this very clear.

> Since therefore the children share in flesh and blood, he himself likewise partook of the same things, that through death he might destroy the one who has the power of death, that is, the devil, and deliver all those who through fear of death were subject to lifelong slavery. For surely it is not angels that he helps, but he helps the offspring of Abraham. Therefore he had to be made like his brothers in every respect, so that he might become a merciful and faithful high priest in the service of God, to make propitiation for the sins of the people. For because he himself has suffered when tempted, he is able to help those who are being tempted. (Hebrews 2:14-18)

In the preceding verse, God's people are referred to as "children" (Hebrews 2:13). The expression "flesh and blood" is a rabbinic expression that refers to our humanness.[26] We need to understand, therefore, that because we are human, it was necessary for God to become human in order to free us from the bondage of sin and death. If his intention had been to redeem the angels, the writer of Hebrews tells us, it would have been necessary for him to become an angel, taking their attributes. That, however, was not his intention; he came to save us. To do that, he had to become like us, the inspired writer tells us, "in every respect."[27] Jesus was totally human; it's our salvation that was at stake.

It's not only important that Jesus was fully human; it also is critical that he was fully God. As we've seen, Jesus claimed to be God and those who knew him best recognized him as God but he also was completely human. Here's why that matters: If Jesus were not human, his death would not apply to us; if he were not divine, it would not have been sufficient to purchase our salvation.

**Let's Talk About It**

- It is so easy for us to assume that our situation is fundamentally different from that which Jesus faced. What implications do you see in the suggestion that Jesus truly faced life as you and I do?

- Jesus faced life as you and I do, yet he lived a perfect, sinless life. If you or I were to receive and act upon the grace (i.e., spiritual help) that God offers to us, does this suggest that we also could live a sinless life, like Jesus? If not, why not? If so, then why aren't we also perfect?

---

[26] This expression is used five times in the New Testament—Matthew 16:17; 1 Corinthians 15:50; Galatians 1:16; Ephesians 6:12; and Hebrews 2:14.
[27] For an exploration of Jesus' example in facing temptation, see Appendix B.

# CHAPTER 16

## Who is Jesus?

"Christ" is not Jesus' last name. If Jesus had a last name it probably was Bar-Joseph (i.e., "Son of Joseph"; cf. Luke 4:22) although he more frequently was identified by his hometown; he was known as "Jesus of Nazareth" (e.g., Mark 10:47). "Christ," actually is a title; it is the Greek equivalent of the Hebrew, "Messiah" (cf. John 1:41). Both of these titles, in the respective languages, are best translated "Anointed."

More than 500 years before the birth of Jesus, Daniel prophesied a coming "Anointed One, a prince" (Daniel 9:25). As a result, there was great anticipation in Israel, waiting for the arrival of this promised "Anointed One," or "Messiah." The elderly Simeon, who had been assured he would see "the Lord's Anointed," recognized the infant Jesus as the fulfillment of this promise (Luke 2:25-32). Jesus' disciples also recognized him as the promised "Anointed One." After meeting Jesus, Andrew excitedly reported to his brother, "We have found the Messiah" (John 1:41). When Jesus asked the disciples who they thought he was, Peter answered for all, "The Christ [i.e., Anointed] of God" (Luke 9:20).

Jesus even claimed to be the promised "Anointed One." When he attended the synagogue in his hometown of Nazareth, he was given the scroll of Isaiah. He opened it to Isaiah 61 and read, "The Spirit of the Lord is upon me because he has anointed me to proclaim good news to the poor" (Luke 4:18). When he finished reading, he returned the scroll to the attendant, sat down (the position of a teacher) and said, "Today this Scripture has been fulfilled in your hearing" (Luke 4:21).

In ancient Israel, anointing with oil (a substance that does not quickly evaporate or disappear) symbolized designation for a holy function or role. Thus, the tabernacle designed for the worship of God was anointed with specially compounded oil (Exodus 30:22-25). Divinely appointed individuals also were anointed, reflecting their designation to a holy responsibility before God. Specifically, prophets were anointed (1 Kings 19:16), priests were anointed (Exodus 30:30), and kings were anointed (1 Samuel 16:1, 11-13). As "the Lord's Anointed," Jesus is the ultimate fulfillment of all of these offices.

A prophet is one who speaks God's word to his people. There were many prophets whom God sent but one of the greatest of the Old Testament prophets was Moses. It was Moses to whom God entrusted his law for Israel. At the end of his life, Moses prophesied that "The LORD your God will raise up for you a prophet like me from among you, from your brothers—it is to him you shall listen" (Deuteronomy 18:15). Nearly fourteen centuries later, Peter declared that Moses' prophecy was fulfilled in Jesus (Acts 3:22-23). The epistle to the Hebrews begins, "Long ago, at many times and in many ways, God spoke to our fathers by the prophets, but in these last days he has spoken to us by [or in] his Son" (Hebrews 1:1-2). The Apostle John also reports, "The Word [or message] became flesh [or embodied] and dwelt among us" (John 1:14). Jesus was the promised prophet and more than a prophet; he not only delivered God's message, he embodied it.

During his lifetime, Jesus was recognized as a prophet by the people who interacted with him and who observed his ministry (Matthew 21:45-46; John 4:19; Lk 7:16). Jesus also identified himself as a prophet, reminding the people of Nazareth that "no prophet is acceptable in his hometown" (Luke 4:24). He refused to be threatened by Herod because "it cannot be that a prophet should perish away from Jerusalem" (Luke 13:33). Furthermore, like the Old Testament prophets, he claimed that his message was from God. He said that he was taught by the Father what he should speak (John 8:28) and that he did not speak on his own authority "but the Father who sent me has himself given me a commandment—what to say and what to speak" (John 12:49).

Like the prophets of the Old Testament era, Jesus also foretold future events. "The Olivet Discourse" (Matthew 24-25) entirely deals with the future. Jesus also foretold the circumstances of his death and his resurrection on the third day (Matthew 16:21).

In addition to prophets, the Old Testament also provided for anointing of priests (Exodus 40:12-15). Although their priesthood was "perpetual," their term of service was limited by their lifespan. David, inspired by God, envisions a priest who serves forever (Psalm 110:4). The writer of Hebrews tells us that David spoke of Jesus (Hebrews 7:15-22).

The role of the priest was to represent people before God in presenting gifts and sacrifices for sin (Hebrews 5:1). Jesus did this, but not by repeatedly offering animal sacrifices which are incapable of taking away sin (Hebrews 10:11). He gave himself, the perfect sacrifice, "once for all" for the forgiveness of sin (Hebrews 9:11-14; cf. 10:12-14). Today, Jesus continues his priestly role as he intercedes and advocates for us before the Father (Hebrews 7:25; 1 John 2:1).

During the Old Testament era, God also commanded that Kings should be anointed. God sent Samuel to anoint Saul as Israel's first king (1 Samuel 10:1-2). After God rejected Saul as Israel's king, he sent Samuel to anoint David as king over his people, Israel (1 Samuel 16:1, 12-13). Zadok the priest and Nathan the prophet anointed Solomon king following the death of his father, David (1 Kings 1:34). Elijah was sent to anoint Hazael king over Syria (1 Kings 19:15). Other examples could be added but anointing clearly was a confirmation of God's choice of one to be king.

The angel's announcement to Mary included the promise that her baby would occupy "the throne of his father David, and he will reign over the house of Jacob forever, and of his kingdom there will be no end" (Luke 1:32-33). The magi also came asking, "Where is the one who has been born king of the Jews?" (Matthew 2:2). Jesus' kingship was rarely recognized during his earthly life. After Jesus gave them food to eat, the crowd was ready to make him king (John 6:15) but Jesus, knowing the crowd was fickle and that his time was not yet, eluded their intent. The same fickleness is seen in the crowd's songs of Hosanna on Palm Sunday, as they chanted, "Blessed is the King of Israel!" (John 12:13). Nevertheless, that crowd was nowhere to be found later the same week when others shouted, "Crucify him!" or when Pilate posted a sign on his cross, "Jesus of Nazareth, the King of the Jews" (John 19:19).

Jesus Christ is the risen and reigning sovereign of the universe. Paul reminds us that "all things were created through him and for him" (Colossians 1:16) and that he "is the head of all rule and authority"

(Colossians 2:10). Although Jesus' initial coming did not bear the majesty or exercise the power of a reigning king, the Scriptures tell us that Jesus will return again "with power and great glory" (Matthew 24:30). John records a vision in which he foresaw the future coming of Jesus.

> He is clothed in a robe dipped in blood, and the name by which he is called is The Word of God. And the armies of heaven, arrayed in fine linen, white and pure, were following him on white horses. From his mouth comes a sharp sword with which to strike down the nations, and he will rule them with a rod of iron. He will tread the winepress of the fury of the wrath of God the Almighty. On his robe and on his thigh he has a name written, King of kings and Lord of lords. (Revelation 19:13-16).

Whether we know him as Jesus of Nazareth or as Jesus Christ, we learn from the Scriptures that he was and is, "The Lord's anointed." He was and is the ultimate fulfillment of the roles of prophet, priest, and king. We, in turn, do well now to heed his message, to receive the gift of his sacrifice, and to submit to his reign in our lives, just as all creation—every person in heaven, on earth, and in hell!—someday will acknowledge him as Lord, as both God and Sovereign of the universe (Philippians 2:10-11).

**Let's Talk About It**

* Is it really important that Jesus fulfilled the roles of prophet, priest, and king? Why?

* In which of those roles do you find the most comfort?

# CHAPTER 17

## Jesus' Death For Us

The death of Jesus for us must be seen as the center point of biblical truth, the fulcrum on which all theological understanding is balanced. Everything we have discussed to this point leads to and prepares us to understand the death of Jesus for us and everything we will discuss in the following chapters flows out of and is the result of Jesus' death for us.

When God chose to expand the circle of his relationships by creating other persons like himself, he had a problem. He knew, before he created anything, that the persons he would create—those we know as people, including you and me—not only must be able to make free choices (just as he does) but also would use that freedom to rebel against him. Rebellion is incompatible with personal intimacy; it is one or the other. To respond justly to his rebellious creatures would require eternal separation from his presence.

In order to realize his desire for an expanded community of relationship, God had to find a way to remove the offense of human sin and to restore his creatures to alignment with his character. The Triune God did this by personally taking the just punishment for our sin into himself. That is the good news in an otherwise hopeless situation. Jesus, the second person of the Trinity, freely became our substitute, taking the penalty for rebellion that we deserve and restoring the possibility of relationship that God desires. Jesus is the reality which all the sacrifices of the Old Covenant anticipate. He is "the Lamb...slain from the creation of the world" (Revelation 13:8 NIV), "the Lamb of God who takes away the sin of the world" (John 1:29). Obviously, this truth needs to be unpacked.

We already have seen that the Bible confirms the fact that every human being is a sinner (Romans 3:10-20, 23); we all are inclined toward sin and repeatedly choose to sin, defying God's commands, profaning his character, and rejecting his gracious offers of spiritual help. Sin is "missing the mark" of conformity to God's character, it is "falling aside" from his will for us, it is "unrighteousness" before a righteous God, it is "stepping over the line" of God's will for us, and it is rebellious determination to pursue a path of our own choosing.

That his creatures sinned did not come as a shock to God; he is omniscient, knowing the things people freely will choose in the future. He knew when he put Adam and Eve in the garden that they would defy his prohibition to eat from the tree in the center of the garden (cf. Genesis 2:16-17; 3:6). He also knew the various ways that you and I would rebel against him in the 21st Century.

When God told Adam that he must not eat from the forbidden tree, he also warned that "in the day that you eat of it you shall surely die" (Genesis 2:17). Death is not just the physical cessation of a heart beat or brain waves; death, ultimately, is separation, the breaking of relationships. When a friend or loved one dies, bodily functions cease but more painful is the loss of relationship, the ability to enjoy the person's presence, to talk and laugh and cry together. We even may think of death as a metaphor for relational alienation and separation. When Adam and Eve sinned, they died; they did not die physically (although they surely would) but they died spiritually, their relationship with God was broken.

When they sinned, Adam and Eve entered the sphere of death; that is the condition into which each of us was born and in which we live, unless we have been "reborn" into God's family. Jesus said that the one who believes his message "has passed from [the sphere of] death into [the sphere of] life" (John 5:24)—from relational alienation to relational intimacy. Paul notes "if, because of one man's [i.e., Adam's] trespass, death reigned through that one man, much more will those who receive the abundance of grace and the free gift of righteousness reign in life through the one man Jesus Christ" (Romans 5:17).

There is more! Not only does our sin consign us to the sphere of death, it also deeply violates and offends God's character, that which is the very essence of his existence as God. We have not sinned simply against our own character or against our friends and neighbors; as David confesses, ultimately our rebellion is directed against God himself (Psalm 51:4). As a result, God is angered by our rebellion. Paul writes,

> The wrath of God is revealed from heaven against all ungodliness and unrighteousness of men, who by their unrighteousness suppress the truth. For what can be known about God is plain to them, because God has shown it to them. For his invisible attributes, namely, his eternal power and divine nature, have been clearly perceived, ever since the creation of the world, in the things that have been made. So they are without excuse. (Romans 1:18-20)

"Wrath" is a strong word, but it is appropriate. God has made his existence clear for everyone to see but still we rebelled—and continue to rebel. Nevertheless, God's wrath is not the penalty for sin. As our first parents were warned in the Garden of Eden and as Paul affirmed in his epistle to the Romans, "the wages [or penalty] of sin is death" (Romans 6:23a), broken relationship, alienation from God.

The offense of our sin needed to be covered, cleaned up, taken away. If our sin remained exposed in God's sight, then God could not accept us. In the Old Testament, God provided animal sacrifices as an "atonement" for sin (Leviticus 1:3-4). The English words "atone" and "atonement" commonly are used to translate Hebrew words that mean "covering." The death of an animal, however, is an inadequate covering; it only is a picture of our need for a covering and is not a substitute for the death we deserve as sinners (Hebrews 10:4).

Furthermore, in rebellion against God, we align ourselves with Satan, the arch-enemy of our very existence. Satan entraps us in patterns of sin that we are powerless to break and that keep us from experiencing God's love. Jesus observed that "everyone who commits sin is a slave to sin" (John 8:34).

So, there we were—all of humanity—in the sphere of death, alienated from God, living under his wrath, totally unable to free ourselves from the downward spiral of death in order to reestablish relationship with a holy God. There, too, was God, loving and desiring fellowship with the rebellious creatures he had created, but also perfectly holy and just. He could not simply turn a blind eye to our rebellion (Nahum 1:3; Habakkuk 1:13). He justly could have damned the entire human race but that would have frustrated his desire to expand his circle of relationships. Furthermore, God loves people; he desires people to return to him, not to destroy them (Ezekiel 33:11; 2 Pt 3:9).

In order to realize his desire, God had to address humanity's sin problem. That's the problem for which Jesus is the solution. In Jesus, the triune God accepted the consequence of our sin. He became a human like us, he faced life as we do, yet without sin (Hebrews 4:14-15), he laid down his life for us (John 10:18), and he rose from the dead that we could be declared just and holy (Romans 4:25), fit companions for a holy God. He delivered us from the sphere of death, he vanquished our enemy, he provided a once-for-all covering for our sin, and he ransomed and redeemed us from a life of futility and bondage to sin.[28]

It is natural to ask how Jesus accomplished all this for us. How is it that he "bore our sins in his body on the tree" (1 Peter 2:24)? We should be cautious when addressing this question since God has not provided specific revelation on this holy topic. Whenever we attempt to probe the divine mysteries, we do well to proceed cautiously and with great humility. It is with caution, therefore, that I offer the following suggestion.

We have noted that physical death is a metaphor for alienation and broken relationship. Certainly, that is the opposite of the relational oneness that has characterized the Trinity from eternity past and that God desires with the persons whom he created. Our rebellious sin frustrates God's desire by offending his character and alienating us from his fellowship. Our condition is hopeless. God, however, graciously chose to accept into himself the alienation we deserve, thus satisfying divine justice by bearing the consequence of our sin (cf. Romans 3:26).

On the cross, merging the reality of physical death with the deeper reality of relational alienation, the oneness of the Trinity was shattered.[29] Jesus, the Second Person of the Trinity, was alienated from the Father and the Spirit. Jesus, is our Savior, having accepted our alienation, but this breach in relationship wounded the Father

---

[28] It often is taught that, on the cross, Jesus bore the wrath of the Father on our behalf but this entails several problems. This suggestion is addressed in Appendix C.
[29] Note that the brokenness suggested is relational, rather than ontological. The Trinity remained a trinity, the three persons sharing a common existence, even when relational oneness and fellowship was sacrificed for our redemption. This is essential, since any rupture in God's ontological oneness would have resulted in the cessation of God's existence and the existence of the universe which he created and sustains.

and the Spirit, as well. It is in this sense that God accepted the consequence of our guilt into himself. This does not diminish the role of Jesus as our Savior but it does expand our comprehension of the effect of our sin and the wonder of Divine grace.

If broken relationships are not healed, they fester with destructive effect. Having accepted our alienation at the cost of Trinitarian oneness, Jesus triumphed over death and alienation, as symbolized by his physical resurrection from death.[30] Jesus' resurrection certifies that the consequence of our sin has been met, that death— i.e., alienation, our ultimate or "last enemy" (1 Corinthians 15:26)— has been conquered, and that Satan, whose purpose it is to alienate and to destroy relationships and who, thus, wields the power of death (Hebrews 2:14), has been vanquished (cf. Colossians 2:15). Jesus not only accepted our alienation and relational brokenness, he surmounted it. In doing so, he not only restored the relational oneness of the Trinity, he provided the one and only way for our fellowship with the persons of the Trinity to be restored.

That the price of our redemption entails acceptance of our alienation into the Trinity may be suggested by Jesus's cry from the cross (Matthew 27:46). Jesus' cry, however, should not be taken (as it often is) to indicate that Jesus was abandoned by the Father or was the object of the Father's wrath. Unlike 21st Century Christians, the ancient Jews memorized passages rather than verses. (The Hebrew Scriptures weren't even divided into verses.) As Jesus hung on the cross, it is reasonable to assume that he meditated on Psalm 22 since his cry is the opening verse of that Psalm. Although the initial cry reflects the pain of alienation and broken relationship, the Psalm, taken as a whole is not a song of abandonment but a song of triumph. Although Jesus experienced deeply the pain of alienation from the Father and the Spirit, he also saw beyond relational brokenness to reconciliation and restoration of oneness. He declared victory over the powers of sin and death. Jesus' death for us entailed a temporary but painful fracturing of fellowship within the Trinity but it is not appropriate to conclude from Jesus' cry that he was the object of the Father's wrath.

Even more helpful in understanding these mysteries are Isaiah's songs of the suffering servant.[31] In these songs, Isaiah graphically describes the work of Christ for us.

[30] It is not my intention to question in any way the reality of the physical resurrection of Jesus. I only note that the physical resurrection also holds deep symbolic and theological significance.
[31] The servant songs are found in Isaiah 42:1-9; 44:1-5; 49:1-6; and 52:13-53:12.

> Surely he has borne our griefs
>> and carried our sorrows;
> yet we esteemed him stricken,
>> smitten by God, and afflicted.
> But he was wounded for our transgressions;
>> he was crushed for our iniquities;
> upon him was the chastisement that brought us peace,
>> and with his stripes we are healed. (Isaiah 53:4-5)

And again,

> Yet it was the will of the LORD to crush him;
>> he has put him to grief;
> when his soul makes an offering for sin,
>> he shall see his offspring; he shall prolong his days;
> the will of the LORD shall prosper in his hand.
> (Isaiah 53:10)

There is no question that these songs find their ultimate fulfillment in the Messiah; Matthew, John, and Peter cite them and apply them to Jesus (Matthew 8:17; John 12:38; 1 Peter 2:24).

I assume that Jesus' post-resurrection walk to Emmaus and his instruction of the Twelve (Luke 24:25-27, 44-47) included an exposition of these songs. That "it was the will of the LORD to crush him," however, reflects no conflict within the Trinity. The redemption of humanity—like the resurrection of Jesus (cf. John 10:18; Acts 2:32; Romans 1:4)—was a choice and provision not of the Father, nor of the Son, nor of the Spirit in isolation, but of the Trinity. The members of the Trinity took pleasure not in the anguish of alienation but in the restoration of fellowship which it accomplished. The Father and the Spirit were pleased by the Son's sacrificial assumption of the guilt of humanity, with its awful consequence—"he was pierced for our transgressions; he was crushed for our iniquities; upon him was the chastisement that brought us peace"—because through it reconciliation between God and humans was provided.

Great, indeed, is the mystery of godliness. As Paul exclaims, "Oh, the depth of the riches and wisdom and knowledge of God! How unsearch-able are his judgments and how inscrutable his ways!" (Romans 11:33).

This is the Gospel, the good news. What we could not do for ourselves because of sin, God has done for us. Jesus—the perfect God-man—took our sin and freely became our substitute. Because he was truly human, the redemption he purchased can apply to us; because he was truly God, his death was adequate to provide redemption for all humanity. Redemption is not automatic, however; it is a gift that must be received. God does not force this gift on us. If we do not receive his gift, accepting that he already has borne the consequence of our sin, the consequence will fall on us (John 3:18). That is not a fate anyone would want to consider (Hebrews 10:31).

**Let's Talk About It**

- I have suggested that "life" and "death" are metaphors for relational wholeness and relational brokenness. What do you think about that suggestion? Why does this suggestion appeal to you or what concerns does it raise in your mind?

- How does it make you feel to realize that the eternal fellowship within the Trinity—the very fellowship into which God desires to draw you—was broken in order to make it possible for you to experience intimacy with God? How would you like to express your sense of gratitude?

# CHAPTER 18

## What's Confusing About Sin and Salvation

We've come a long way so it would be good to stop for a recap. Our earth and everything in it was created by a perfect, personal, all-powerful, all-wise, and loving God who desired to expand the circle of his fellowship. In order to realize that desire, he chose to create other persons like himself whom we know as humans. Even though our capacities are limited in comparison to his, we are like him in that we can know, can experience joy and grief, can make meaningful choices, and can relate to others, including to him.

As we've seen, given the option of continuing in relationship with him or violating that relationship in quest of self-promotion, our first parents (and each of us, since) chose to rebel. This did not take God by surprise. He knew before he created us that this is the course we would choose and that the result would be fatal—fatal to us and fatal to his desire to expand the circle of his relationship.

Therefore, he did what we could not do. He accepted the limitations of humanity in order to become one of us and he, himself, accepted the punishment—the rupturing of relationship—that is the consequence of our rebellion. Furthermore, having entered into our alienation, he healed it. As a result, he can and does offer us reconciliation and renewed fellowship with himself. Those humans who accept this offer can experience growing intimacy with God and others now, and will enjoy perfect and eternal fellowship with God, as he desires.

Christians throughout the ages have understood this story although most people either have accepted or rejected it without trying to articulate the underlying truth as a coherent system. Throughout the early centuries of the Christian Era and the Middle Ages, distinctions were clarified by church leaders as they responded to aberrations of biblical truth. The focus of most devoted Christians, however, was on entering deeply into relationship with God.

One aberration advanced by Pelagius, a 4th Century British monk, held that the human will was not affected by the fall into sin and, therefore, without God's help people can choose what is good, including to embrace salvation in Christ. The effect of his teaching was to discount the need for God's grace.

Augustine of Hippo led the church's response to Pelagius's teaching. Augustine was trained in Platonic philosophy and taught "rhetoric" (i.e., debate) prior to his mid-life conversion to Christianity. Following his conversion he entered the priesthood and was appointed Bishop of Hippo, a significant city on the Mediterranean coast of current-day Algeria. Augustine argued that the Bible teaches the human will is enslaved to sin and that God's grace is essential to any right choices, including the choice of salvation. Augustine's case was persuasive and "Pelagianism" was condemned as heresy at the Council of Carthage in A.D. 418.

The issue of the human will, however, naturally raises questions about God's will. Augustine recognized that God is both perfectly omnipotent and perfectly just. Since not all people are good and just—indeed, all of us are sinful and some clearly are reprobate—this posed a problem for Augustine. If goodness is contingent on God's grace, why has God not extended grace to all?

Augustine specifically struggled with 1 Timothy 2:4: "[God our Savior] desires all people to be saved and to come to the knowledge of the truth." Since God is omnipotent, he should be able to obtain whatever he wishes, but all people are not saved. In the end, Augustine was unable to resolve this apparent conflict. After proposing a couple less-than-satisfying suggestions, his final answer was to affirm that "we may interpret [1 Timothy 2:4] in any other way we please, so long as we are not compelled to believe the omnipotent God has willed anything to be done that was not done."[32] In his thinking, therefore, the meaning of the verse is secondary to the doctrine of God's omnipotence.

Furthermore, if God could have extended saving grace to all but did not, is this not unfair? Because God's omnipotence and justice

---

[32] Augustine. *Enchiridion*. In Nicene and Post-Nicene Fathers. Philip Schaff, ed. Peabody, MA: Hendrickson Publishers. Vol 3, p 103.

appear to be in conflict, Augustine had to address the issue of God's justice. He argued that God is justified in damning every human because all have sinned and deserve damnation. Since God has no obligation to save any, however, he is free to extend mercy to some without compromising his justice. In doing so, he has assured the salvation of some and the damnation of the rest. Augustine described this as "predestination."[33]

Thomas Aquinas, an Italian friar who lived in the 13th Century, is distinguished for his work in developing what may be considered the first Christian "systematic theology." Aquinas drew together the doctrines affirmed in all the church Councils and the teachings of Church leaders across the centuries, including the work done by Augustine. In doing so, Aquinas cited and advocated Augustine's views on providence and predestination.[34]

In the 16th Century, when Martin Luther (a German, Augustinian monk) declared his stand for faith alone as the basis of salvation, the Reformation was launched and the church was forever changed. Luther did not systematize his theology, however; he was too occupied with exploring and describing the extent of human sinfulness and the nature of God's grace. As a result, Lutheran theology, even today, holds in tension the biblical themes of "Law" and "Gospel."

The task of developing a protestant systematic theology fell to a Frenchman, Jean (or John) Calvin, a contemporary of Luther, although twenty-six years his junior. Calvin was a pastor and apologist at heart. He did not set out to write a systematic theology. Rather his desire was to lead his people to a mature understanding of the Gospel, evidenced in a truly Christian community, and to win the king of France to embrace the Gospel of grace. Although Calvin was a prolific writer, his greatest work is his *Institutes of the Christian Religion*. In it, he presents a systematic description of biblical truth as he understands it. It is a marvelous description of Christian truth that continues to influence the thinking of many.

Like Augustine and Luther, Calvin was captivated by the thought of an almighty, absolutely omnipotent, and sovereign God who extends grace to fallen men and women. Calvin was, first of all, a student of the Scriptures. He knew that all humans stand guilty before God and that salvation is dependent entirely on God's grace.

---

[33] *Ibid.*, p 100.
[34] Thomas Aquinas. *Summa Theologica*, First Book, Questions 22, 23.

He also understood that God has chosen those he will redeem and that God's choices (he called them "decrees") are unchangeable. He did not move beyond Augustine, however, to an understanding of the relationship between God's choices and human choices.

Embedded in the story of aspiration, tragedy, and redemption with which we began this chapter is a profound mystery: How can it be that humans (people like you and me) can make real choices, choices that deserve commendation or incur guilt, when all of creation is ruled by an almighty, sovereign God? From the time of Augustine, but especially since John Calvin, the most common answer to that question has been that we cannot know. Sometimes referred to as an "antinomy" (i.e., a violation of the laws of logic) or a mystery (i.e., something beyond human understanding), the relationship of God's sovereignty to our human capacity to choose typically is dismissed as unknowable.

Certainly, there is much that God has not chosen to reveal to us (Deuteronomy 29:29), but the truth of both God's sovereignty and humans' capacity to make meaningful choices for which they are held accountable is clearly taught in the Bible. If this means that God and I both are responsible for a specific choice, we have a huge problem. Two agents cannot be equally and independently responsible for the same decision.[35] That's a problem because God has taught us that consistency—rational and empirical—is the test of truth. If God's sovereignty and our capacity to make free choices—choices that bring God pleasure or incur our guilt— is irrational, then one, the other, or both is not true and we are obligated to reject it.

Although Augustine and Calvin never resolved the problem of God's sovereignty and our human capacity to make real choices (typically referred to as "human freedom"), it is possible for us to understand how these relate.

The first task is to clarify how we use the terms "divine sovereignty" and "human freedom." If "divine sovereignty" is defined as "God's control of everything," then the problem cannot be solved. If sovereignty is defined as "God's right to control everything," however, the problem disappears. God is seen to be "sovereign over

---

[35] This suggestion is proposed by some who argue for "dual agency" or "concurrence" (e.g., Wayne Grudem, *Bible Doctrine*, Grand Rapids: Zondervan, 1999, pp 143-151). Grudem acknowledges the problem inherent in his position, although he affirms it, nonetheless.

his sovereignty." He can choose when to exercise his sovereignty and, if he so chooses, when not to exercise it.

It also is important to understand what we mean by "human freedom." Although we may assume we are absolutely free to choose and do as we wish, that is a huge misperception. In fact, we have no control over most of the things that shape our lives. We have no choice over the century, culture, or family into which we are born. We have no choice over most of the circumstances of our lives. And we have no choice over the persons who enter our lives.

Nevertheless, we do have control over three very important things: (1) We can choose how we will use the time, talent, and treasure that God entrusts to us; (2) We can choose how we will respond to the circumstances in which we find ourselves; and (3) we can choose how we will relate to the persons who enter our lives, including God, himself. In these areas, God has chosen to withhold the exercise of his sovereignty in order to allow us to make real choices—choices for which he justly holds us accountable.

Sin complicates this picture because, as sinful humans, we are irresistibly drawn to egocentric and self-destructive choices. Fortunately, God's response is to provide amazing grace—spiritual help that enables us to do what is right and what he requires of us. He does not force us to accept his offer of grace, and often we do not. Nevertheless, his offer of grace always is adequate to overcome our tendency to turn away from him. Paul put it eloquently:

> No temptation has overtaken you that is not common to man. God is faithful, and he will not let you be tempted beyond your ability, but with the temptation he will also provide the way of escape, that you may be able to endure it. (1 Corinthians 10:13)[36]

The fact of God's sovereignty and human freedom, therefore, is not the problem it may appear. God is totally, 100% sovereign over everything in the universe; he has the right to determine everything that happens. In most cases (thankfully!) he exercises that sovereignty. He controls the circumstances of our lives and directs the course of human history.

Nevertheless, in his relationship with human beings—created in his image as persons with the capacity to make meaningful choices

---

[36] For an elaboration of the significance of this verse, see Appendix B.

that change their lives and the world in which they live—God has chosen to limit the exercise of his sovereignty. With respect to the use of our time, talents, and treasure, to our response to the circumstances in which we find ourselves, and to our relationship to the persons God brings into our lives (including himself), God allows us to choose freely. He extends to us grace needed to make right choices but he does not force us to choose what is right. He does, however, hold us accountable for the choices we make. Often bad choices lead to suffering for ourselves and others but decisions to reject God's grace in favor of our egocentric pursuits also can lead to estrangement from him and eternal separation from his presence.

While understanding God's sovereignty, human freedom, sin, and grace resolves much of the confusion that has plagued theologians throughout the centuries, there remain the biblical teachings of God's election, or choice of those who will experience salvation, and of "predestination." Consumed, as he was, by God's majesty and sovereignty, Calvin followed Augustine in teaching that God, prior to creation and based only on his sovereign will, chose those who will be saved and that his choice is certain and unchangeable. That, however, leads to the conclusion that my response to grace ultimately is irrelevant; God will save whom he has chosen and the rest of humanity will be damned. Those who follow Calvin today deny that this conclusion is inevitable. They know the Scriptures teach that our choice to accept God's grace is significant but how or why is a mystery.

Again, carefully defining the words we use holds the key to understanding. "Election" simply means "to choose" or "choice." The basis of the choice is not implied in the term itself. Calvin and his followers assume that election is a sovereign act of God, influenced by nothing outside himself. If that is the case, however, how is it just—and the Bible clearly teaches that God is just (Deuteronomy 32:4; Romans 9:14)—for God to hold me accountable for a decision he made apart from me?

At this point, we need to recall that God is sovereign over his sovereignty, that he can choose when he will exercise his prerogative to determine events and when he will allow us, humans created in his likeness, to make choices which he will accept. We also need to recall that God is omniscient, that he knows everything, including all that is past, present, and future, all possibilities and actualities, and all determined and free events.

It is reasonable and appropriate, therefore, to recognize that God has chosen ("elected") to save those whom he knew, even before the moment of creation, would accept his grace and own him as their Lord and Savior in the 21st Century. That he knew this is a function of his omniscience; it implies no limitation or constraint. Thus it does not violate my freedom to embrace or reject the grace that he offers nor does it diminish in any way my responsibility for the choice that I make. When I embrace his grace, the glory belongs to him (since I would not have chosen rightly apart from his grace). When I reject his grace, the guilt belongs to me (not only because I am the rebel but also because I could have accepted God's help and made the right decision had I so chosen). In no case is God surprised by my choice, although he may be grieved by it. His foreknowledge of my choice enabled him unerringly to choose me, in Christ, before creation.

"Predestined" is a biblical term (Acts 4:28; Romans 8:29, 30; Ephesians 1:5, 11). The root word implies certainty regarding the choice made; God's election, indeed, is certain. The prefix, "pre," implies that God's election was certain prior to some subsequent event. Ephesians 1:4 states that God chose us prior to creation and, thus, prior to any decision by you or me.

Calvin assumed that God's "decrees," including his choices regarding the salvation or damnation of all people, are made independently, purely as an exercise of his sovereignty. Why, however, must sovereignty preclude access to God's omniscience? Why, specifically, would God choose to ignore his omniscience when determining the salvation or damnation of those he created for relationship with himself? For Calvin, the answer rests in his understanding of God's sovereignty. Any consideration other than God's independent choice is viewed as diminishing his sovereignty.

If my salvation was determined by God's choice prior to creation without reference to his omniscience (specifically, his knowledge of future, free, actualities), then my sense of making meaningful choices (including my response to God's grace) is a mirage, and I cannot justly be held accountable for the choices I make. If, on the other hand, predestination refers to God's settled choice, prior to creation, to relate to me on the basis of his foreknowledge of the choices I make in the 21st Century, then God is completely sovereign and clearly just, and I am fully accountable for my response to his grace.[37]

Aren't you thankful the Scriptures clearly teach that God desires the salvation of all (1 Timothy 2:4; 2 Peter 3:9) and that the salvation purchased by Christ is sufficient for all (1 John 2:2), even though salvation must be appropriated by faith (Ephesians 2:8-9)? Confusion about God's sovereignty, human freedom, election to salvation, and predestination is unnecessary when we carefully understand the terms by which these concepts are expressed.

### Let's Talk About It

- I have suggested that carefully defining the words we use can help us sort out the confusion that often surrounds discussion of sin and salvation. Why is this so important?

- In a previous chapter we observed that God does not always get what he wants. How does resolution of the apparent conflict between divine sovereignty and human freedom illustrate that point? Why is it important for our significance (as persons created in God's image) and for our salvation?

---

[37] The alternative perspective suggested here often is associated with a Dutch theologian, Jacob Arminius. For a discussion of Calvinism and Arminianism, see Appendix D.

# CHAPTER 19

## God's Chosen People

Rome conquered Greece in 146 B.C. Despite the military outcome of the Battle of Corinth, however, it would be easy to argue that Greece conquered Rome. The Romans adopted Greek architecture, arts, philosophy, and worldview, and ancient Hellenic culture continues to shape Western thinking to this day. In contrast to the nations around them, the Greeks embraced "individualism"—a perspective that values the individual and his or her interests over those of the community. When individuals prosper and are fulfilled, individualism assumes the community will prosper, as well. This perspective is pervasive in our Western cultures.

The contrasting social perspective, known as "collectivism," holds that the value of each individual is embedded in his or her relationship with and care for others, that all should pursue the interests of others and of the community above their personal interest. Ancient Hebrew culture, like traditional cultures today in the non-Western world, shared this collectivist perspective. Collectivism has obtained a bad name from its identification with atheistic Marxism. Communism, however, is a hierarchical, power-distorted aberration of collectivism. Biblical priority on family, neighbor, community, and nation has little in common with atheistic Communism.

Cultural perspectives tend to function like colored glasses, without our awareness tinting all that we see. The individualism/collectivism distinction is a case in point. We do well to keep this in mind as we think about God's chosen people.

The previous chapter briefly traced the history of Christian thought regarding grace, election, and predestination. We noted that the triune God, "chose us ... before the foundation of the world, that we should be holy and blameless before him" (Ephesians 1:4). Thus, the Bible teaches that God, in eternity past, chose (or elected) to save those whom he foreknew would embrace his gracious offer of salvation. Our election is individual and personal.

The words omitted when quoting Ephesians 1:4, above, were "in him"—God "chose us in him [i.e., in Christ] before the foundation of the world...." We need to understand what it means to be chosen "in Christ" and to what extent our election is collective.

In the Old Testament, "Israel" is both the name of a person—the new name that God gave Jacob (Genesis 32:28)—and the name of a nation. The promises given to and the covenant made with Abraham were repeated to his son, Isaac, and his grandson, Jacob (i.e., Israel) and were fulfilled (partially, at least) in the nation God had promised would come from Abraham's line. The promises were given to an individual and to all those identified with him.

As Paul explains, identity was not determined by physical descent, however, but through shared faith in the One who had given the promises (Gal 3:6-9). In his letter to Christians in Rome, Paul argues "not all who are descended from Israel belong to Israel" (Romans 9:6). Those who inherited the promises given to Abraham, Isaac, and Jacob were those who emulated and shared the faith of the patriarchs rather than simply those who shared their gene pool. The Israel of God is determined individually, yet the real Israel— the one that inherited the promises—is a "remnant," a community, within national Israel.

The "Servant Songs" of Isaiah[38] address and describe one whom God says is "my Chosen" (Isaiah 42:1; 44:1; cf. 49:1). The songs are addressed to Israel (Isaiah 44:1; 49:3), to the faithful remnant within national Israel, but also are Messianic, finding their greater fulfillment in Jesus Christ (cf. especially, Isaiah 53:1-12). The Chosen One is prefigured in the life of the many and the many are included in the life of the One.

In the New Testament, Jesus is the Chosen One of God (Luke 9:35); Matthew specifically states that "the Chosen One" of Isaiah 42 is Jesus (Matthew 12:15-21). Jesus is "chosen and precious" (1 Peter 2:4), qualities which were prophesied in Isaiah 28:16 (1 Peter 2:6). As those identified with Christ and members of his community,

---

[38] See Isaiah 42:1-4; 44:1-5; 49:1-6; and 52:13-53:12.

believers—individually and collectively—participate in his election. We are "a chosen race, a royal priesthood, a holy nation, a people for his own possession, that [we] may proclaim the excellencies of him who called [us] out of darkness into his marvelous light" (1 Peter 2:9).

In Romans 5, Paul makes a similar point regarding the believer's identification with Christ. Paul sets Jesus in contrast with Adam. Each, he suggests, is the head of a race. Those who are members of Adam's race—i.e., the community identified with Adam—share Adam's bondage to sin and death; those who are members of the new race—the new community, of which Jesus is head—share Jesus' righteousness and eternal life (Romans 5:12-21).

Certainly individual believers are elected by God (cf. Romans 8:29-30). I am awed by the fact that the eternal, omnipotent, and perfectly holy God desires a personal, intimate relationship with me! Nevertheless, we are elected into a relationship that is both individualistic and communal. When Paul writes, "he chose you," the "you" is plural (1 Thessalonians 1:4; 2 Thessalonians 2:13-15; cf. Romans 8:31-39; 11:5, 7, 28). It is Christ's church (Matthew 16:18; Ephesians 5:23), Christ's body (1 Corinthians 12:12-27),[39] Christ's bride (Ephesians 5:25-27) that is chosen to be holy (Ephesians 1:4; 2:21) and radiant (Ephesians 5:31-32; cf. Revelation 21:2, 9-11). In John's vision of heaven, the multitude before the throne is not just a crowd of individuals, it is a redeemed community, praising the Lamb (Revelation 7:9-10).

It is not insignificant that the metaphors God uses to describe the church are the metaphor of a bride (Revelation 19:7) and the metaphor of a city (Revelation 21:9-11). The metaphor of marriage, of a bride and groom, speaks of intimacy, of depth of relationship. The metaphor of a city speaks of multiple networks of interdependent relationships. God's vision for his people centers on relationship!

If we are to live out this reality now, it cannot be in isolation but as a people, a holy nation, a priestly kingdom in the service of God (1 Peter 2:9-10). Relationship is important, not only with God but also with his people, his church, local and global. The mark of Christians is that they love one another (John 13:34-35). The mark of the church is its collective ministry of mutual up-building (Ephesians 4:11-16; cf. Colossians 3:12-14; 2 Thessalonians 1:3-5). Our

---

[39] Compare Romans 12:4-5; 1 Corinthians 10:16-17; Ephesians 3:6; Colossians 1:18.

identity, individually, is with Christ and with this community that God has chosen "in Him" (Ephesians 1:4, 7, 11, 13).

Recognizing God's choice to save me causes me to marvel at his amazing grace. Recognizing that Jesus is "the Chosen One" and that I am vitally related to a community that is "chosen in Him" causes me to fix my gaze on Christ, shifting focus from myself, and to celebrate, nurture, and extend this community which defines my identity.

**Let's Talk About It**

- How does individualism shape our perception of ourselves and of others? How does it tend to order our priorities and determine our focus? Identify two or three areas of your life and think about individualistic and collectivist implications for your behavior and relationships in those areas.

- How do you respond to recognition that you are "elect in him"—in Christ? What do you need to do in light of this recognition?

# CHAPTER 20

## Turning Around

If you're headed in the wrong direction and you know it, usually the smartest thing is to take the first opportunity to turn around.

The word "conversion" has acquired technical meaning in the Christian lexicon but the New Testament word behind it actually is commonly used in everyday speech. It means, simply, "to turn around." When a hemorrhaging woman, in the press of a crowd, secretly touched Jesus' robe, Jesus "turned around" to see who had touched him (Mark 5:30). Also, when John, the elderly apostle exiled to Patmos, heard a loud voice like a blast from a trumpet, he "turned around" to see who was speaking (Revelation 1:12).

In its more technical sense, the word "conversion" appears only once in the New Testament; Paul visited various churches "describing in detail the conversion of the Gentiles" (Acts 15:3). The verb form of the word appears nearly forty times, however, so the idea represented has an important place in New Testament thought.

In both the Old Testament and the New Testament it is common to picture humans, in their sinful rebellion, as walking away from God. Obviously, what is needed is for people to "turn around," to be converted. On the steps of the temple in Jerusalem, Peter called the crowd that had gathered to "Repent therefore, and turn [around], that your sins may be blotted out, that times of refreshing may come from the presence of the Lord, and that he may send the Christ appointed for you, Jesus" (Acts 3:19-20). When persecution caused believers to scatter from Judea, some went to Antioch where they shared the Gospel "and a great number who believed turned to the Lord" (Acts 11:21). As Paul wrote to Christians in

Thessalonica, he rejoiced that they had "turned to God from idols to serve the living and true God" (1 Thessalonians 1:9). This act of "conversion," of "turning around," is the fundamental response God requires of us if we are to enjoy a relationship with him.

As we study God's call for us to turn to him, we see two distinct aspects of conversion. The first is "repentance" (cf. Acts 3:19, quoted above). The New Testament word translated "repentance" literally means "to change one's mind." In the Bible, the term always appears in the context of moral unrighteousness, so it means "to change one's mind about sin." The result of this change of mind always is to turn around, turning away from sin.

The message of Jesus was similar to that of John the Baptist in that both called people to repent (Matthew 3:1-2; Mark 1:14-15). When Jesus sent the twelve out to preach in the villages of Galilee, they "proclaimed that people should repent" (Mark 6:12). When some asked about others who had been victims of a natural disaster, Jesus exposed their assumption that the tragedy had occurred as punishment for sin. He made the point that those who asked also needed to repent (Luke 13:1-5). In Athens, standing before the intellectual giants of his day, Paul declared that God "commands all people everywhere to repent" (Acts 17:30). Refusal to repent can be tragic. Jesus "denounced" the cities of Chorazin and Bethsaida, where most of his miracles had occurred, because they did not repent (Matthew 11:20-21).

Jesus instructed his disciples (including us) to forgive a Christian brother or sister who sins against us and repents (Luke 17:3-4). Recognizing repentance (in ourselves and others), however, can be tricky. It's especially tricky when a person is "caught" in their sin. Obviously, repentance entails more than saying, "Sorry." We need to recall that repentance is "changing one's mind" and includes "turning around," abandoning the sinful behavior that is the reason for repentance.

One way to discern true repentance is to reflect on one's own behaviors when unrepentant. When I sin, the first thing I want to do is to hide my sin so others will not be aware of it. If my sin becomes known, however, my second tactic is to attempt to avoid the consequences of my sin. (I assume you can identify with this.) So, when someone confesses[40] sin—whether it's myself or someone

---

[40] Note the derivation of the word "confess"—"con" means "with" and "fess" means "to speak." Thus, to "confess" is to say the same thing about my sin that God says.

else—the first thing I look for is to see if the person still is trying to hide the wrong that was done. If he is, that is not encouraging. If the person acknowledges that she has sinned but tries to avoid the consequences of her sin, that also is not a good sign.

The consequence of some sins is natural (e.g., those who abuse substances can end up with fried brains). Other sins, however, bear consequences that must be imposed by the state, by the church, by parents, or by the Christian community. Jesus teaches us, when repentance is real, we are free to do as our Father in heaven and forgive the sinner. This, actually, can be a powerful testimony. The watching world knows how to "get even"; it does not understand forgiveness and grace.

The first aspect of conversion is repentance but "changing one's mind," abandoning the sinful behavior, is not sufficient by itself. The second half of conversion is turning to God. Not only does God require us to reject our old, sinful way of living, there also must be an attitude of trusting Christ (or, we might say, entrusting ourselves to Christ). The apostles had one Greek word for this, but our English Bibles use two words to translate it. The verb translated "to believe" and the noun translated "faith" really are forms of the same Greek word. The writer of the letter to Hebrew Christians reminds us that "without faith [or belief] it is impossible to please God" (Hebrews 11:6).

Just as saying "Sorry" is not repentance, acknowledging that God exists is not the faith God requires. James warns us that "even the demons believe—and shudder!" (James 2:19). On the other hand, one need not have a comprehensive understanding of biblical truth to be accepted by God. Indeed, some with very flawed understandings of God's revelation are, nevertheless, accepted by him. (Aren't you thankful your acceptance by God is not determined by a theological test?) It is important, therefore, to understand what is the "faith" or "belief" that God requires.

Although acknowledging the truth of God's revelation does not exhaust the meaning of biblical faith, it is an essential starting point. To ignore or deny reality is not biblical faith. The last half of

God says, "This is sin"; I say, "Yes, this is sin." God says, "Because this is sin, you stand guilty before me"; I say, "Yes, I stand guilty before you." God says, "Because you are guilty, you deserve to be punished"; I say, "Yes, I deserve to be punished." Thankfully, God is merciful to those who confess their sins, who say the same thing about them that he does. He assures us, "if we confess our sins, he is faithful and just to forgive us our sins and to cleanse us from all unrighteousness" (1 John 1:9).

the verse from Hebrews, cited above, instructs us, "whoever would draw near to God must believe that he exists and that he rewards those who seek him" (Hebrews 11:6).

Faith which pleases God must begin with intellectual acceptance of the truth, but it also must include personal confidence in God and willingness to trust him to do those things which he has promised. As Jesus neared the end of his ministry, he became more explicit in teaching his disciples. Mark records his instruction about prayer which also included instruction about faith that God requires and honors.

> Jesus answered them, "Have faith in God. Truly, I say to you, whoever says to this mountain, 'Be taken up and thrown into the sea,' and does not doubt in his heart, but believes that what he says will come to pass, it will be done for him. Therefore I tell you, whatever you ask in prayer, believe that you have received it, and it will be yours." (Mark 11:22-24).

God expects us not only to acknowledge the reality of his existence as God and the truth of his revelation in the Bible and in the life and ministry of Jesus, he also requires us to place our confidence in him, to trust him to do what he has promised.

Acknowledging God's truth and trusting his word, however, still does not exhaust the meaning of biblical faith. John connects "believing" with "receiving" Christ (John 1:12). To receive a person is to welcome him or her. John cannot mean literally to receive Jesus as a guest in one's home, since that was not an option for those to whom John wrote. Jesus had ascended to heaven at least fifty years before John penned these words. Biblical faith does require "receiving," or welcoming, Jesus as the Lord and master of one's life. To those who receive him—"who believe on his name"[41]—John assures us, Jesus gives "the right to become children of God" (John 1:12).

In addition to acknowledging, trusting, and receiving, however, biblical "faith" also includes obeying. Hebrews 11 often is referred to as "God's hall of faith," since the chapter recounts so many Old Testament saints who were shining examples of faith. Careful study of this chapter, however, reveals that the men and women whose

---

[41] In Hebrew culture, a person's name was equivalent with his or her person, with his or her character. Thus, to "believe on [Jesus'] name" was to accept him for who he claimed to be, God incarnate and the Savior of all who place their faith in him.

stories are highlighted not only believed God, they trusted him and acted on the basis of what they believed (cf. Hebrews 11:8). What a challenge for us, today, who profess faith in God! Biblical faith shapes life.

Earlier we noted that humans are egocentric sinners who naturally choose that which is self-destructive and evil, contrary to the character of our holy God. Presented, therefore, with God's call to turn around, we inevitably plunge headlong toward our own destruction. In a later chapter we will examine the Bible's teaching about grace. At this point, we just need to note that "grace" is spiritual help that God extends to us which enables us to do what he requires of us. So, with his call to turn around, God enables us to do so. We can accept or reject his help but if we reject God's grace we cannot plead that we lacked the opportunity or capacity to turn around and embrace God's gift of restored relationship with himself.

"Turning around," including both repentance and faith, is the basis for God's forgiveness of our sin and for establishing the intimate relationship he desires with us. This is a truth we dare not ignore. Peter's message to Cornelius (and to us) was, "everyone who believes in him receives forgiveness of sins through his name" (Acts 10:43). Paul testifies, "I am not ashamed of the gospel, for it is the power of God for salvation to everyone who believes" (Romans 1:16). Even more ominously, John warns, "Whoever believes in him is not condemned, but whoever does not believe is condemned already, because he has not believed in the name of the only Son of God" (John 3:18). We don't need to do anything to be condemned by God; we all naturally start there. It only is those who "turn around," who repent of their sin and place their faith in Jesus Christ who are pardoned, received into God's family, and extended the privilege of intimacy with God.

This truth requires self-examination but it also motivates witness. When we understand that all our friends and neighbors who do not know Jesus, all those who cross our path but do not know him, all those who live in societies where the good news about Jesus is unknown, that all these are "condemned already," we understand why the Great Commission (Matthew 28:19 20) is not just a casual suggestion. It's all about turning around.

**Let's Talk About It**

- How often have you found yourself trying to hide the wrong you have done or trying to avoid the consequences of your actions? How does this help us understand God's perspective on our claims of repentance? How can this help you as you lovingly try to lead others to repentance regarding their self-destructive behaviors or lifestyle?

- I have suggested that "believing" necessarily entails acknowledging, trusting, receiving, and obeying. Why is each of these essential to "faith"? Think about these responses one at a time: How would "faith" be affected if any of these responses were omitted?

# CHAPTER 21

## The Big Change

I had the privilege of being at L'Abri, in Switzerland, in 1971, when Francis Schaeffer (a missionary pastor and Christian apologist) preached his mother's funeral message. In that setting, he noted that it is common to consider death the great transition, a transition from this life to the afterlife (or, for naturalists, from existence to non-existence). For the Christian, Schaeffer observed, death is not the great transition; our conversion is. When we "turn around," acknowledging Christ as our Lord and Savior, we transition from the realm of death to the realm of life. Physical death is a lesser transition—from living with Christ here to living with Christ in heaven.

When a person, enabled by God's grace, responds to God's call to "turn around," God joyfully performs a miracle in the life of that person that the Bible describes in several ways. One way is in terms of the community that defines one's identity. The person is transferred from Adam's community, characterized by death (temporal and eternal), to Jesus' community, characterized by life eternal.

Another way to view this miracle is in terms of the change God creates in the person herself or himself. Before turning around, one naturally chooses paths of self-destructive sin; after turning around, God provides a new desire for God and his ways. This change is so dramatic that Jesus refers to it as being "reborn" (John 3:7).

Yet a third way to view the miracle that occurs is in the way God views the person. Before turning around, God rightly pronounces a person guilty of sin and condemned to eternal punishment. After turning around, God pronounces the person's guilt forgiven—the penalty paid by Jesus—and the person as sharing the righteousness of Jesus Christ. Clearly, all these ways of understanding God's miracle in the life of the believer need to be explored.

The first way the Bible describes this miracle is as realignment of our identity. In his letter to Christians in Rome, Paul observed that when Adam our first parent sinned, a death penalty—as well as a human nature infected by death—was passed to the entire race of which Adam is the "head" (i.e., the first or source). As Paul put it, "Just as sin came into the world through one man, and death through sin, and so death spread to all men because all sinned…" (Romans 5:12). Paul then identifies a second Adam, Jesus, as head of a new race (Romans 5:14; cf. 1 Corinthians 15:45-49). When a person "turns around," God changes her or his identity. No longer is a person's primary identity in Adam's race. God welcomes the person into the new race, the new community, of which Jesus is head.

The "Adam" with which we are identified, to whose community we belong, is critically important, as Paul points out. "For if, because of one man's trespass, death reigned through that one man, much more will those who receive the abundance of grace and the free gift of righteousness reign in life through the one man Jesus Christ" (Romans 5:17).

This new identity effects profound change. As nihilistic philosophers remind us, Adam's community is haunted by meaninglessness imposed by impending death. Jesus' community, on the other hand, experiences purpose and meaning because we participate in his life. To the Christians in Colossae, Paul writes, "He has delivered us from the domain of darkness and transferred us to the kingdom of his beloved Son, in whom we have redemption, the forgiveness of sins" (Colossians 1:13-14). In this, Paul echoes the words of Jesus, "Truly, truly, I say to you, whoever hears my word and believes him who sent me has eternal life. He does not come into judgment, but has passed from death to life" (John 5:24).

A second way the Bible describes the miracle God preforms in the life of the person who "turns around" is expressed as a new beginning. Paul wrote to Titus about "the washing of regeneration and renewal of the Holy Spirit" (Titus 3:5). Of the two words Paul uses to describe this change—"regeneration" and "renewal"— "regeneration" is the more interesting because it is less familiar.

To "generate" means to create or to bring into existence. (A "generation" is those people who were brought into existence, or were born, at about the same time.) "Regeneration," therefore, means to begin anew. The only other time this word is used in the New Testament (Matthew 19:28) the ESV translates the word "in the new world" (i.e., the new heavens and the new earth in which Jesus will establish his Kingdom) and the NIV translates the word "at the renewal of all things." That suggests the magnitude of the change God creates in the life of the new believer.

Paul seems to search for ways to express this change. Writing to Christians in Corinth, he said, "if anyone is in Christ, he is a new creation. The old has passed away; behold, the new has come" (2 Corinthians 5:17; cf. Galatians 6:15). Writing to Christians in Rome, he described the effect of this change as "new life" from God the Holy Spirit (Romans 7:6). In his letter to Christians at Ephesus, Paul used the metaphor of resurrection to describe this change. Originally, he said, "you were dead in the trespasses and sins in which you once walked" but God "made [you] alive together with Christ" (Ephesians 2:1-6). Jesus implied all of this when he told Nicodemus, "You must be born again" (John 3:7).

Closely related to the metaphor of rebirth is the metaphor of adoption. Paul told the Galatian Christians that Jesus was born and died "so that we might receive adoption as sons" (Galatians 4:4-5). As children in God's family, God gives us his Spirit "by whom we cry, 'Abba! Father!'" (Romans 8:15; cf. Galatians 4:6). As God's children, we are heirs to the riches of God in Christ and to unending life with him (Romans 8:16-18; Titus 3:4-7).

This change is seen in several ways. It affects my mind; now I understand God's truth whereas, before "turning around," spiritual truth was just nonsense (1 Corinthians 2:14-16; cf. Colossians 3:10). It affects my will; whereas previously I naturally did what is evil, now God works in me, by his grace, "both to will and to do" his good pleasure (Philippians 2:13 KJV). This change also affects my desires; whereas previously I was "alienated from the life of God" (Ephesians 4:18), now although I have not seen him, I love him. I enjoy being with him and delight in him (cf. 1 Peter 1:8). God has implanted his love in my life, so I now love him and I love his people (1 John 4:19-5:1).

A third way the Bible describes the miracle God performs when a believer "turns around" is by contrasting our past and present standing before God. Because we are members of a new community and, indeed, have a new identity in Christ, God relates to us differently. As members of Adam's race, we stood condemned before him (John 3:18). As members of Jesus' race and children in God's family, Jesus' death has paid the penalty of our sin (Romans 5:6-11). God sees us in the righteousness of Jesus and declares us holy (1 Corinthians 6:11). The term the Bible uses for this is "justification"; we are "justified by his blood" (Romans 5:9).

"Justification" is an interesting word. It does not cause a change; rather, it declares a condition that already exists and is observed. Luke tells us that those who heard Jesus commending the ministry of John the Baptist "declared God just" (Luke 7:29—literally, they "justified God"). What the people said did not change God's reality—he is eternally just—but they recognized that God is just and declared him to be just. We also see how this word is used in Jesus' observation that "Wisdom is justified by her deeds" (Matthew 11:19), a person is proven, or declared, to be wise by the way she or he lives. We also see this when Solomon warns, "He who justifies the wicked and he who condemns the righteous are both alike an abomination to the Lord" (Proverbs 17:15). Saying that evil is good does not make it good—a reality that many in our relativistic culture overlook to their own peril.

So, when God "justifies the ungodly" (Romans 4:5), he is not stating an untruth or indulging a "legal fiction." He declares us just, forgiven, and holy because that really is our new identity. God no longer views the members of Jesus' race in the sin and guilt of the first Adam but in the righteousness of Jesus Christ. God looks at me and sees Jesus because I am united to him as a member of his new race, his community. Because he sees me in Jesus, he is right to declare me just and holy. That's my new reality as a member of Jesus' community. (There is more to say about alignment of my life with this new reality, but we'll discuss that in following chapters.)

The bottom line is this: Salvation begins with God as he calls us to turn around and extends to us grace needed to do so. It continues with God as he responds to our repentance and faith by adopting us into his family, by giving us a new nature, and by declaring us just and holy in Christ. As we will see, salvation always will be of God since we are dependent on his grace as we pursue relationship with him throughout this life and as we worship and serve him throughout eternity. May his name be praised!

**Let's Talk About It**

- What do you think of Schaeffer's suggestion that the moment of "turning around," of repenting for sin and placing faith in Christ, marks a bigger transition than dying? Why do you agree or disagree?

- Nicodemus was totally confused when Jesus told him "unless one is born again he cannot see the kingdom of God" (John 3:3). Does the term "born again" communicate any better to our generation? How would you like to express the truth behind Jesus' words?

# CHAPTER 22

## Amazing Grace!

There are few songs as well known in the English-speaking world as John Newton's wonderful hymn, "Amazing Grace." The words of "Amazing Grace," supported by the beautiful melody that carries them, are recognized and sung by Christians and non-Christians, alike. Although many speak of "grace," we do well to ask what the Bible means by "grace."

When asked to define "grace," some suggest, "God's Riches At Christ's Expense." It's a clever acronym and easy to remember, but I don't find it particularly helpful in understanding the meaning of "grace." You also may hear "grace" defined as "unmerited favor." I find that more helpful, although it may make it difficult to distinguish "grace" from "mercy."[42]

In an earlier chapter, "grace" was defined as spiritual help which God extends to us that enables us to do what he requires of us. It only is as we do what he requires of us that we can experience God's favor. God is holy; he only can receive those who are holy as he is. That standard is impossible for me to attain by myself; I am a sinful person. In order to be holy, like God, I need help—lots of help! God has met my need in two ways: First, he rescued me from my sinful condition and placed me in Jesus' community where I receive the holiness of Jesus. Second, God "graces" me by enabling me to make right choices—choices aligned with his will and his righteousness. Living a holy life really is possible for me! There is

---

[42] The New Testament word translated "grace" (*charis*, χάρις) is part of a word group that comes from a root that indicates "things which produce well-being." Well-being, in this context, typically results from a gift (cf. *charisma*, χάρισμα—"spiritual gift") and, thus, reflects favor (*charizomai*, χαρίζομαι) toward the recipient and indicates that the one so gifted is favored (*charitoō*, χαριτόω). As used in the New Testament, "grace" typically is an act of God which is intended to bring people into his favor.

much to say about both of these ways God offers grace to us. We need to back up and start from the beginning.

In summarizing "the big change" that God makes in the life of the believer, I suggested that salvation begins with God. That's the only way possible, since it is impossible for humans, marred and bound by sin, to restore our relationship with God. God created us, however, to share intimacy with himself. To realize that goal—to reestablish relationship with his rebellious creatures—God chooses to enable us to respond to his call to repentance and faith. He didn't have to do this, he could have damned the entire human race but that would have frustrated his desire to widen the circle of his relationships. So he reaches out to us, calls us to return to relationship with himself, and offers us the help we need to respond to his call.

God's help is extended to each person in unique ways but everyone is given the help needed to respond to God's call.[43] Although it is common to identify a moment of "conversion," turning around occurs at a particular point in a longer—sometimes much longer—process. You may find it helpful to think of our coming to Christ as a courtship in which our loving God always makes the first move. We embrace (or resist) that move, followed by another move on God's part which we, again, embrace or resist. God is incredibly patient as he seeks to win us to himself.

As you've probably observed, each time we embrace God's offer of grace, it becomes easier to embrace it again and each time we resist God's grace, it becomes easier to resist his grace again. As we embrace God's grace, greater grace is given. In this way we grow in our understanding and are drawn to his offer of reconciliation and intimacy with himself. Similarly, repeated resistance and rejection of grace can result in becoming callused toward God's offers of spiritual help (Romans 2:4-5). The Bible warns there comes a point at which God gives up the rebellious person to the destruction he or she has chosen (Romans 1:24, 26, 28).

It is important to understand the nature of grace as we reflect on the intimacy which God desires and to which he calls us. God is holy—he is perfectly just, pure, and truthful (Isaiah 5:16). He is completely separated from evil. Evil cannot exist in his presence (Habakkuk 1:13). Therefore, he commands us to be holy and he can accept us into relationship with himself only

---

[43] Regarding God's grace to those without access to the Good News, see Appendix E.

as we are holy (1 Peter 1:15-16). Left to ourselves, our situation would be hopeless but God offers us the holiness which he requires. When we "turn around," he does this by including us in Jesus' community. In this way we benefit from and participate in Jesus' holiness. We are blessed "in the Beloved"—i.e., in Jesus (Ephesians 1:6).

God also extends to us grace—spiritual help—needed to live lives of holiness now (Philippians 2:13). Even with the big change that God makes in us when we "turn around," we still have the capacity to resist his grace and the sad truth is that we often do (cf. Romans 7:14-24). As we grow in grace and in our relationship with God, we learn that God's grace enables us to experience victory over temptation and sin (2 Corinthians 3:17-18). This is the mark of maturity in Christ (Ephesians 4:11-15). Nevertheless, no one can claim to have attained holiness in this life (1 John 1:8).

Whenever we choose sin, it always is because we resist the grace offered, never because God's grace is insufficient (1 Corinthians 10:13). Jesus lived a perfect life, not because he is God—remember, he willingly faced life exactly as we do (Hebrews 2:17)—but because he is the only human who consistently embraced the grace offered to him (Hebrews 5:7-9). Thus, his perfect life proves both that God's grace is sufficient and that we are culpable for our failure to embrace his grace and to live the life of holiness made possible by grace.

God's interaction with us as he extends grace is a beautiful reminder that he respects his image in us, including the capacity he has given us to make meaningful choices. God desires me to choose to experience unhindered intimacy with him but he will not violate his image in me by overruling my will and forcing me to choose him. He could do that but he won't; he desires relationship with those who freely choose intimacy with him.

Because God respects his image in us, it is possible for a person to choose to resist God's grace at any point, both before and after "turning around." Those who resist grace before turning around "are condemned already" (John 3:18), not because God's grace was inadequate but because they chose to reject God's offers of spiritual help. Even after "turning around," Christians may resist God's grace, choosing rather to sin. When that occurs, it is important to recognize what we have done, to confess our sin, and to receive God's forgiveness so our relationship with him can be restored and can continue to grow (1 John 1:9).

Each occasion when we resist God's grace is critical, since as we've seen, grace resisted is more easily resisted when we are tempted again. If a pattern of resisted grace is allowed to develop, the consequences can be serious. The Scriptures warn that deliberate sin can lead to apostasy, a condition in which a person intentionally rejects the salvation provided by Christ and renounces his or her place in Christ's community (Hebrews 10:26-31). This cannot happen unconsciously or accidently; "turning around" never is unconscious or accidental and neither is apostasy. Rejection of Christ must be chosen. When chosen, however, the effect is final, no recourse remains (Hebrews 6:4-8).[44] This is why we seek to be sensitive to the Spirit's voice, to quickly confess sin, and to grow in relationship with Christ. We do not want to risk a path of rejected grace that could lead to a tragic end.

The believer who receives and embraces God's grace for daily living, however, who confesses and repents of his or her sin, and who seeks to live in obedience to Christ, has nothing to fear; she or he is held securely by God (John 10:27-30; cf. 2 Peter 1:10). Nothing in all creation can separate that believer from Christ (Romans 8:38-39). This is the confidence we enjoy as children in God's family.

---

[44] It is not surprising that both references cited to support the possibility of apostasy come from the New Testament letter to Hebrew Christians. This letter was written to a community that was weighing the option of rejecting their faith in Christ and returning to Judaism. The letter, therefore, specifically addresses the issue of apostasy. The two passages cited are not unique; warnings also are given in Hebrews 2:1-4; 3:12-15; 12:12-17; and 12:25-29. The possibility of apostasy also is seen in the Old Testament's denial of forgiveness to the one who sins "with a high hand" (i.e., arrogantly, intentionally, defiantly—Numbers 15:29-31; cf. Ezekiel 18:23-26). Warnings against apostasy specifically are included In Jesus' parables of the soils (Luke 8:11-15), the abusive manager (Luke 12:42-46), and the vine and the branches (John 15:1-6). Paul often encourages his readers to remain faithful to Christ (1 Corinthians 9:24-27; 10:1-12; 11:28-32; Galatians 6:7-9; Philippians 3:12-4:1; Colossians 1:21-23; 1 Timothy 1:18-20; 4:1-3; 6:9-12). Significantly Paul reminds Timothy that "if we deny [God], he also will deny us...for he cannot deny himself" (2 Timothy 2:12-13)—i.e., God cannot violate his own character by ignoring someone's denial of him.

## Let's Talk About It

- I have suggested that "grace" is "spiritual help which God extends to us that enables us to do what he requires of us." How does this help us distinguish "mercy" from "grace"? Why do you need both mercy and grace?

- How have you seen, in your own experience, that grace received and applied leads to more grace—i.e., temptation loses its attraction—while grace rejected results in a pattern in which it becomes increasingly easy to sin? What implications do you see in this for your pursuit of intimacy with God?

# CHAPTER 23

## Being Sure

I grew up as the son of a Baptist pastor in a small town in central Kansas. I first attended church when I was exactly two weeks old; our family's life centered on the life of the church and its programs. TV had not yet reached central Kansas in the 1940s and the rhythms of life were tuned to the farming cycle. That was a wonderful environment in which to spend my formative years.

One Sunday evening when I was six years old, the Lord spoke to my heart through the Gospel visually portrayed in Christian baptism. As my father explained the significance of dying with Christ and being raised to newness of life in him, I knew that is what I desired. I did not share my desire immediately but the next morning, before going to school, my father led me in a prayer of confession and acceptance of Christ as my Lord and Savior.

Not surprisingly, my life changed little as a result of my conversion. Perhaps for that reason, in my early teens I began to question whether I really was a Christian. When I was fourteen years old, I shared my doubts with my father. I love the memory of my father but on that occasion he failed me. Rather than taking me to the Scriptures to show me God's provision for being sure, he simply said, "Of course you are a Christian." End of discussion.

That did not satisfy my doubts. About two years later, a Christian life speaker came to my school and I made an appointment to meet with him. I shared my doubts with him and asked for his guidance. His response was to say, "Well, if it didn't work the first time, let's just get down on our knees and pray the sinner's prayer again." I did, but I did not leave that room with greater assurance than when I entered.

I enrolled at Wheaton College when I was seventeen. I majored in Bible and spent every Sunday at a mission outreach in the Chicago slums. All the while, I continued to wrestle with questions about my salvation that had plagued me since my early teens. Gradually, my doubts began to spread, first to the truth of Christianity and, ultimately, to the existence of God, himself. Nevertheless, I continued in my Bible major and in my mission work in Chicago.

In my junior year in college, God met me in a very special way. During the spring semester I had a theology course in which we studied the doctrine of salvation and, at the same time, I was enrolled in a course on the Epistle to the Hebrews. Hebrews was written to a community of Christian Jews who were tempted to reject their faith in Christ and return to Judaism.

One very cold winter Sunday afternoon, while engaged in my mission work in Chicago, I knocked on the door of a shack built under Chicago's "L" (elevated railway) tracks. A little, old, African-American woman opened the door and I asked her if she would like to have a Bible study. To my amazement, she said she would love to study the Bible, so I was faced with the responsibility of identifying material I could use for a Bible study with her.

The next week, back in Wheaton, I went to a local Christian bookstore and perused available Bible study books. I chose one on 1 John; it was only five chapters long and looked like something that would enable me to fulfill the commitment I had made with minimal effort. What I did not know at the time was that John wrote this epistle, guided by the Holy Spirit, specifically to answer the question of assurance of salvation. John states his purpose clearly:

> I write these things to you who believe in the name of the
> Son of God that you may know that you have eternal life.
> (1 John 5:13)

I will never know what that little African-American woman got from our Bible studies together but God used those studies, together with my courses in theology and Hebrews, to answer my questions and provide me with assurance of salvation. For the first time in my life, I was sure!

When I continued my study of theology in graduate school, I wrote my master's thesis on "The Basis of the Believer's Assurance of Present Salvation: A Historical Study in the Theologies of John

Calvin and John Wesley."[45] I chose the topic because I anticipated an interesting contrast between Calvinistic and Arminian responses to the issue of assurance of salvation. I was wrong. Both Calvin and Wesley were so much men of God's Word that their positions were almost identical.

Since then, I have learned that it is common for children raised in Christian homes who accept Jesus as their Savior at an early age to face a crisis of faith in their teen years or later. God does not intend, however, for his children to live in doubt and fear; he intends for us to be sure. I will share my understanding of God's Word about being sure, but I encourage you to make your own study of the Epistle of 1 John. Make your own list of references in this short book on the topic of being sure and study those verses in context to identify the evidence God identifies for testing our faith and grounding our confidence.

If you do that, I believe you will see that John identifies two evidences on which to establish our confidence. The first is the believer's changed life. Christians "keep his commandments" (1 John 2:3)—they obey the teaching of the Bible. Christians "walk in the same way [Jesus] walked" (1 John 2:5-6)—they follow Jesus' example by seeking to please God in all things. Christians "practice righteousness" (1 John 2:29; 3:10)—they choose to do what is right before God. This may not result in immediate behavioral change but it certainly does mean that one's core values and heart desires are reoriented. Pursuit of one's own interests is replaced by desire to know and please Christ. This never happens naturally; it only can be supernatural. Naturally, we are egocentric; when God performs the miracle of rebirth, he gives us new desires—specifically, a desire to know and please him. This change is a clear sign that a person is a child of God. We don't immediately become perfect and we do continue to be tempted and to sin, but the direction of life changes and that change is an appropriate basis for assurance of salvation.

The second evidence of salvation that John provides is mentioned first in 1 John 3:24. I refer to this as a "hinge verse," since both bases for assurance of salvation are mentioned here. John writes:

> Whoever keeps his commandments abides in God, and God in him. And by this we know that he abides in us, by the Spirit whom he has given us. (1 John 3:24)

[45] Wheaton College Graduate School, 1965.

Note that the word "Spirit" is capitalized. Here and in the second half of his letter, John points the believer to the testimony of God's indwelling Holy Spirit as a basis for being sure (1 John 4:13). Paul also reminds the Roman Christians that they have received the Holy Spirit "by whom we cry, 'Abba! Father!'"[46] and that "The Spirit himself bears witness with our spirit that we are children of God" (Romans 8:15-16).

We should not expect to hear a voice from God; rather, the Spirit of God draws us into an "Abba! Father!" relationship with God in which we experience God's love, security, and inner peace. When Christ reigns as Lord of one's values and desires, he brings freedom (John 8:36) and peace with God (Romans 5:1). There is an end to struggle and effort to please him that comes with knowing we are accepted in Christ. Life takes on new meaning. As John writes, "Whoever has the Son has life; whoever does not have the Son of God does not have life" (1 John 5:12).

In a clear reference to Jesus' description of himself as "the good shepherd" (John 10:1-18), Calvin notes that Christ "willingly offers himself as shepherd, and declares that we shall be numbered among his flock if we hear his voice."[47] We long to hear the voice of our shepherd and as we hear it we are drawn to him. Our desire for Christ and our experience of him as the guardian and shepherd of our lives assures us that we are accepted in Christ.

There are two ways, therefore, that those who have trusted Christ can be sure—the external testimony of a changed life and the internal testimony of the Holy Spirit. There are many ways to look for assurance of salvation, however, that are not found in Scripture. Another person's opinion is not a reliable way to be sure. (Remember my father's response to my questions?) Simply praying the sinner's prayer a second (or third, or tenth) time also is not an effective way to be sure.

Sometimes those seeking assurance of salvation are encouraged to place their name in John 3:16. They might be advised to say, "For God so loved Jim (or Jane) that he gave his only Son, that if Jim believes in him, Jim should not perish but Jim should have eternal life." Thus, "Jim" (or Jane) is encouraged to accept John 3:16 as a way to be sure "based on the authority of the Bible." This may appear to

---

[46] "Abba" is an Aramaic word of intimacy and endearment, roughly equivalent to the English terms "Papa," or "Daddy." Jesus' mother language was Aramaic.

[47] John Calvin. *Institutes of the Christian Religion*, Book 3, 24, 6.

be good advice but it will not survive careful reflection. The doubting person soon realizes that the "authority" trusted is not the Bible but one's own insertion of his or her name into the text.

Others may encourage the doubter to look back to the moment he or she accepted Christ. I have read advice to pound a nail in a tree to remind one of the time of her or his salvation. More common is encouragement to write the date of one's salvation in a Bible. Then, when doubts about one's salvation arise, the doubter can go back to the nail in the tree or the date in one's Bible to be reminded of their moment of salvation. This, too, is a basis of assurance that cannot satisfy. Upon reflection, the doubter realizes that any assurance derived rests on his or her own judgment that the faith expressed in that moment was saving faith. Scripture never points the believer to a past experience as the basis of assurance of salvation.

As we have seen, however, Scripture does offer two, clear ways to be sure. As you examine your life before the Lord, do you find that the direction of your life has changed? Do you desire to obey God and to be like him? Furthermore, as you observe your heart, do you experience a peace that comes from oneness of heart and mind with God's Holy Spirit and from knowing Christ as your guardian and shepherd? If this is your experience, then the Bible says you can be sure. You are free to embrace Christ, who has saved you from an egocentric life, and to celebrate the joy he provides as you grow in obedience to and intimacy with him.

## Let's Talk About It

- I mentioned that it is not uncommon for those raised in a Christian family to experience a crisis of faith in their teen years or later. Has this been your experience? If so, what did you find most helpful in this chapter? If your experience is different, have you also wrestled with doubts regarding your salvation? What have you found most helpful in dealing with your doubts?

- Doubts tend to spread; remember how my doubts began with my salvation but grew into questioning the truth of Christianity and even the existence of God? Why is that? How does this underline the importance of addressing swiftly and biblically the doubts that Satan raises in our minds? Can you relate a personal experience that illustrates this?

# CHAPTER 24

## Growing In Intimacy

"Being sure" is important, but it is not God's greatest desire for us. We often have noted that God's purpose in creation was to expand the circle of his relationships. Relationship—especially intimate relationship—must be reciprocal; one person cannot create an intimate relationship without the willingness and help of the other. We rarely think of God's limitations but this is one. He cannot and will not form an intimate relationship with someone who is unresponsive or hostile. For God to realize his desire of intimacy with me, I must share his desire and take steps—enabled by his grace and guided by his Word and Spirit—to pursue that relationship.

We already have seen that intimacy with a holy God is possible only as we are holy, as he is. Although, after "turning around," we benefit from the holiness of Christ as members of his community, God also expects us to accept the grace he offers us to think and act and relate to others in ways that are pure and holy. This happens only as we choose to embrace his grace. Paul describes this as growth toward spiritual maturity, defined as "the measure of the stature of the fullness of Christ" (Ephesians 4:13). For a long time that expression made no sense to me. Then, one day, I realized Paul is challenging me to measure my spiritual growth against the standard provided by Christ, in his full maturity. As we often do with growing children, he might have said, "Stand back-to-back with Jesus. Let's see how spiritually tall you are compared to him." How is it possible for me to achieve that standard? It only is possible by God's grace, and even then, none of us perfectly achieves it in this life.

Nevertheless, we cannot be satisfied to live in defeat and sin. Jesus came to give us abundant life (John 10:10), to set us free from the tyranny of sin and death (Romans 8:1-4). By the power of his death and resurrection, Jesus makes available to us grace needed to experience victory over temptation and sin (1 John 5:3-5). Christ intends his people to grow in holiness. This is essential if we are to grow in intimacy with God. Holiness of life also attracts attention from those who do not know Christ and validates our witness.

It seems there are two approaches to living the Christian life. One begins with acceptance that sinless perfection never will be attained in this life and settles for cycles of failure and confession. The other begins with acceptance of the adequacy of God's grace. With trust in God to shield me from temptation that is greater than I can bear (1 Corinthians 10:13), with commitment to obey Christ in every situation, guided by the Scriptures and the Holy Spirit, growth in holiness is expected. We do not expect to attain sinlessness in this life but we do expect increasing victory over temptation and growth in Christlikeness. The first approach yields a Christian life marked by immaturity, mediocrity, and defeat; the second yields a life marked by victory in Jesus as we trust and obey him.

There can be little doubt which perspective Paul embraced. To Christians in Corinth he wrote:

> Do you not know that in a race all the runners run, but only one receives the prize? So run that you may obtain it. Every athlete exercises self-control in all things. They do it to receive a perishable wreath, but we [discipline ourselves to receive] an imperishable [reward]. So I do not run aimlessly; I do not box as one beating the air. But I discipline my body and keep it under control, lest after preaching to others I myself should be disqualified. (1 Corinthians 9:24-27)

And writing to Christians in Philippi, Paul affirmed his supreme desire and his singular commitment to know Christ and to receive Christ's approval for a life well lived. Paul stated the goal of his life:

> That I may know him and the power of his resurrection, and may share his sufferings, becoming like him in his death, that by any means possible I may attain the resurrection from the dead. Not that I have already obtained this or am already perfect, but I press on to make it my own, because Christ Jesus has made me his own. Brothers, I do not consider that I have made it my own. But one thing I do: forgetting what lies behind and straining forward to

what lies ahead, I press on toward the goal for the prize of
the upward call of God in Christ Jesus. (Philippians 3:10-14)

The victorious Christian life is one of dependence and discipline,
discipline and dependence. As we depend on Christ to provide
grace and as we discipline ourselves to receive and act upon the
grace that Christ provides, we can experience growth in grace and
victory over sin. Indeed, we must not settle for less.

God does not intend, however, for us to pursue this life of holiness
alone. A spiritual friendship with a Christian brother or sister of
one's own gender can be very beneficial in our journey toward a
life of victory and maturity in Christ.

A spiritual friendship is unlike even the "best" friendships commonly
experienced. It is not based on shared interests at work, in sports or
hobbies, in politics, or even in Bible study or theological discussion.
Spiritual friendship conversations do not focus on the joys and
stresses of daily life, on one's health (or lack of it), on one's financial
needs or those of loved ones, or on fulfilling or stressed relationships
in the family, in the neighborhood, at work, or in the church. The focus
of Spiritual friendship conversations is the work of God in my life in
the midst of—or in response to—all of these events, circumstances,
and experiences.

Too often relationships are built on pretense and politics; we
pretend to be the person we want to be or we do what is politically
correct, even when it does not reflect our true self or our values.
To have a Christian brother or sister who is committed to you
and to your spiritual growth is invaluable. When we consider our
propensity to be deceived by our own flesh and by Satan's wiles,
our need for a spiritual friend who can help us see ourselves truly
and who will encourage us as we respond to the work of God in
our lives, is a great blessing.

Forming and maintaining spiritual friendships is a discipline that
requires intentionality. The spiritual friend is a brother or sister who
shares one's commitment to spiritual growth and who is able and
willing to speak truth into one's life, whether that takes the form
of encouragement and support or the form of challenge or even
warning. The primary role of my spiritual friend is to help me see
my heart and God's working in my life more clearly. My role is to
reciprocate with insights that will build my friend's obedience to
and intimacy with Christ.

God may grace you with two or three spiritual friends, but it is wise to initiate only one spiritual friendship at a time. Attempting more may prove too stressful both for your schedule and for your emotions. When initiating a spiritual friendship relationship, I naturally look to my circle of friends to identify a brother or sister of my own gender who shares my thirst for spiritual growth and divine intimacy. Especially with a new spiritual friendship, it is wise to commit to a specific time—for example, three months—after which the spiritual friendship can be discontinued or extended. During this time, you should agree to meet for at least an hour, once every couple weeks. A quiet place, conducive to deep conversation, will be a great advantage.

In preparation for a spiritual friendship appointment, review God's work in your life in the preceding weeks. If you keep a journal, you will want to review it. What has God spoken about to you? How have you responded to the word of Christ? How do you see God working through the circumstances of your life to conform you to the image of Christ? How are you responding to God's work through those circumstances? Make notes for yourself of things you want to share with your spiritual friend. Mutual openness and trust are essential. Spiritual friendship cannot thrive if friends are less than honest with one another. The purpose is to be a friend—always listening deeply, frequently questioning or even probing, occasionally offering observations, and sometimes sharing the load of burdens—in order to support the friend's commitment to spiritual growth.

There is no doubt that God desires us to grow in holiness, in a life marked by Christ's victory over sin and temptation, but holiness is not the end for which we were created. We were created for relationship—ultimately with himself but also with his people.

God desires intimacy with us. He desires to speak his truth into our lives as an expression of his loving desire to protect us from evil and to guide us into his truth. He desires us to spend time in his presence, enjoying the beauty of his person, hearing his word to us, and aligning our heart with his. This requires discipline. Enabled by his grace, our disciplined attentiveness and obedience is the doorway to the intimate relationship with God for which we were created and in which we find our ultimate fulfillment.

Intimacy with Christ does not occur naturally; our culture ("the world"; 1 John 2:15-16), our self-destructive preference for evil ("the flesh"; Galatians 5:19-21), and our mortal enemy ("the devil"; Ephesians 6:11-12) oppose it. Because God desires intimacy with us, he extends grace needed to resist these forces and to experience the intimacy he desires. Nevertheless, we also have a part. He calls us to embrace his grace (Hebrews 12:15), to submit ourselves to his Word (1 John 2:4-5), and to seek to know him intimately. Most Biblical Christians recognize the importance of a daily time of quiet reading and reflection on God's Word. Not all reading of Scripture, however, cultivates intimacy. In this regard, I have found helpful the discipline of "attentive reading." I commend it to you, as well.[48]

Intimacy with God may be the ultimate purpose for which we were created but relational health naturally includes others, as well. As we have seen, God intends his people to be a loving community—a community that contrasts sharply with the egocentric, oppressive, and often cruel cultures of this world. The visible expression of that community is the church. (We will consider the Bible's teachings about the church in the next two chapters.) American churches too often emphasize participation in programs, rather than building community. Corporate worship and teaching have value but community is nurtured only in more intimate and stable relationships.

Christian community is not exclusive or cliquish (James 2:1); all who know Christ are embraced. The stranger, also, is treated with dignity, as one who bears Christ's image, and every effort is made to meet his or her needs in ways that are respectful and caring (cf. Matthew 25:31-46). Acts of kindness are love in action. Love for Christ, for other Christians, and for the stranger is the mark of the Christian (John 13:35). This attracts the attention of the watching world and lends credibility to witness.

Do you long to live a life of holiness before God, do you desire intimacy with Him? These are God's desires, as well (Matthew 11:28-30). He calls you to a life of holiness and intimacy with himself. He extends to you the grace—the spiritual help—needed to realize these aspirations but he also expects you and me to embrace his grace, to obey his Word, and to exercise the discipline required to experience the holiness and intimacy toward which we aspire. This does not come instantly but growth In holiness and growth in intimacy is normal in the life of the Christian. How "normal" are you?

---

[48] For suggestions on an approach to "Attentive Reading," see Appendix F.

**Let's Talk About It**

- An old song says, "Trust and obey, for there's no other way to be happy in Jesus than to trust and obey." What do you think of the theology of that song? What is the role of faith and obedience in the Christian life? Is happiness the goal of the Christian life? Where is true happiness found?

- Has your Christian life tended to be cycles of failure and confession or can you recognize a pattern of growth toward holiness and spiritual maturity? What do you think of the suggestion that God's grace, if consistently embraced, is sufficient to enable a Christian to live a life of victory over temptation and sin?

# CHAPTER 25

## God's Family

God has a big family! It may not seem that way, at times, as Christians find themselves at odds with popular culture or with hostile faiths or with governments, but the reality is reflected in Scripture.

> After this I looked, and behold, a great multitude that no one could number, from every nation, from all tribes and peoples and languages, standing before the throne and before the Lamb, clothed in white robes, with palm branches in their hands, and crying out with a loud voice, "Salvation belongs to our God who sits on the throne, and to the Lamb!" (Revelation 7:9-10)

That reality is not visible today[49] but the reality exists, nonetheless. Christians all over the world anticipate the day when that reality will become explicit and together we will be part of that "great multitude."

Today, we experience a microcosm of that reality in the church. The church as we know it was born in the Book of Acts, but we never will understand the full significance of the church if we limit our study to the New Testament. The church is not the same as Israel and yet there is a close relationship between Israel in the Old Testament and the church in the New Testament. God chose Israel to be "a treasured possession"—a people of his own (Deuteronomy 7:6-8; 14:2)—but his love for Israel did not deter him from requiring his people to demonstrate their love for him. If Israel truly was to be the people of God, he expected them to confirm the

---

[49] Large international meetings of Biblical Christians, however, may provide a foretaste of the extent of God's family.

covenant which he made with them by obeying him and honoring his covenant (Exodus 19:5-6).

God is not fixated, however, on rule-keeping (Romans 4:13); his desire is for loving relationships with people who respond to him in faith (1 John 4:9-10). From creation, God's desire and intention to call out a people for himself was global (Genesis 3:15; 12:2-3). The Mosaic Law, Paul tells us, was a "guardian"—a family servant who brought children to their tutor—to bring Israel to faith in Christ (Galatians 3:24). God chose Israel to be "a light to the nations" (Isaiah 49:6). God's people—both in the Old Testament and today—are a spiritual community, not an ethnic or national community. They are known by their faith response to God (Romans 4:16-25; Galatians 3:7-9).

During his ministry, Jesus announced the "kingdom," or reign, of God (Mark 1:14-15; Acts 1:3) and charged his disciples to do the same (Luke 9:1-2). He also told the disciples, "on this rock I will build my church" (Matthew 16:18). (The "rock" referred to is the rock-solid truth that Jesus is the promised Messiah, the Son of the living God—cf. Matthew 16:16-17.) The word "church" has a very specific meaning for Christians but the Greek word adopted by early Christians to speak of their community was a common word for "assembly" and it is used that way, as well as with its more technical meaning, in the book of Acts (see Acts 19:32, 39, 41).

From the book of Acts and from the letters of Paul we can learn much about the life of the church in the 1st Century as it grew from a band of disciples huddled in a locked room (John 20:19) to a brotherhood spread across the Roman Empire (cf. Romans 15:17-24). With the first major expansion of the church, on the Day of Pentecost, Luke records, Christians "devoted themselves to the apostles' teaching and the fellowship, to the breaking of bread and the prayers" (Acts 2:42). Each of these activities is significant if we are to understand the life of the church.

The first, "the apostles' teaching," focuses attention on the instructional function of the church. The ministry of teaching has been an important function since the day God began to call out a people for his own. Israel had not yet left Egypt when God commanded them to teach their children about the deliverance he would provide (cf. Exodus 12:24-27). Before Moses died, he gave God's law to the priests and commanded them to read it to the people, that all Israel may "learn to fear the Lord," to obey

God's law, and to teach their children to know and obey God's law (Deuteronomy 31:11-13). Jesus' "Great Commission" is to make disciples—i.e., learners—and to teach them, not only to recall but, "to observe [i.e., to obey] everything I have commanded you" (Matthew 28:20). When Paul lists the qualifications for church leaders, one is that the leader must be "able to teach" (1 Timothy 3:2; 2 Timothy 2:24). It is because God's revealed truth is important that teaching is an essential aspect of church life.

Fellowship, or community life, also is an important function of the church. Often when we use the word "fellowship" we think of being together and having a good time. The most common meaning of the Greek word translated "fellowship," however, is "identification with someone" or "participation in something." Paul presses this meaning when he writes, "Is not the cup of thanksgiving for which we give thanks a participation in the blood of Christ? And is not the bread that we break a participation in the body of Christ?" (1 Corinthians 10:16). In both cases, the word translated "participation" is the one commonly translated "fellowship."

The "fellowship" of the early church began with mutual identification—a sense of belonging to one another—but it did not stop there. Because I am identified with other believers, their cares are my cares and their troubles are my troubles. Paul reported that Christians in Macedonia and Achaia "have been pleased to make some contribution [literally, "fellowship"] for the poor among the saints in Jerusalem" (Romans 15:26). In this case, "fellowship" meant participating in their poverty. This community life, characterized by identification with and participation in the lives of Christian brothers and sisters is the essence of love; it is the love which Christ said would distinguish his followers (John 13:35).

The third activity of the church mentioned in Acts 2:42 is "the breaking of bread." While this could refer to the simple act of sharing their meals, it probably refers to observance of the Lord's Supper (cf. 1 Corinthians 11:23-26) and, thus, to the gathering of believers for worship. When we worship, our attention is focused on God, on affirming his greatness and glory, on submission to his authority, on entering and enjoying his presence. Worship can include teaching (cf. Acts 20:7), words of admonition or encouragement (e.g., testimonies of God's faithfulness), singing (cf. Colossians 3:16), and collections for the less fortunate (cf. 1 Corinthians 16:2). Times of collective worship also are an essential function of the church.

The fourth and last activity of the early church mentioned in Acts 2:42 is prayer. As the disciples waited for God's empowering, they prayed (Acts 1:13-14). When threatened, they prayed (Acts 4:23-31). When Peter was imprisoned, the church prayed (Acts 12:5). When the church in Antioch commissioned its first missionaries, they prayed (Acts 13:3). When the church in Ephesus said goodbye to Paul, they prayed (Acts 20:36). Paul urged the church to pray (1 Thessalonians 5:17; 1 Timothy 2:1, 8). Since it is God alone who is able to accomplish anything of spiritual value through us, prayer also is an essential function of the church.

In addition to being communities characterized by spiritual teaching, loving relationships, worship of God, and fervent prayer, churches also celebrate baptism and the Lord's Supper. Although the Catholic Church teaches that these (and five other) "sacraments," or holy rites, are means by which God confers grace on observant worshippers, Protestant Christians understand these celebrations differently. While some denominations (e.g., Anglicans, Lutherans, Methodists, and Presbyterians) retain the language of "sacrament," those in the Anabaptist tradition (Mennonites, Baptists, and most Pentecostal and Independent churches) refer to these as "ordinances," or authoritative commands.

Jesus' disciples baptized many who followed him (John 4:1-2) and his Great Commission included a command to baptize those who become disciples (Matthew 28:19-20). Baptism in the name of Jesus was an important celebration in the early church (Acts 2:38; 10:47-48).

Although the word translated "baptize" or "baptism" means to immerse, the early church apparently was quite flexible in practice. A 2nd Century document titled "The Teaching of the Twelve Apostles" (also known as "The Didache") instructs that baptism should be observed by immersion in cold running water (e.g., a river). If cold running water is not available, however, a series of options are listed that include immersion in still, cold or warm, water or pouring.[50] Paul's teaching on the meaning of baptism, however, supports the method of immersion since it dramatically reflects the acts of burial and resurrection. To Christians in Rome, Paul wrote,

---

[50] "The Didache." Translated by J.B. Lightfoot. http://www.annomundi.com/bible/didache.pdf Accessed May 26, 2018.

> Do you not know that all of us who have been baptized into Christ Jesus were baptized into his death? We were buried therefore with him by baptism into death, in order that, just as Christ was raised from the dead by the glory of the Father, we too might walk in newness of life. (Romans 6:3-4)

Rather than viewing baptism as a means of grace, most Protestant Christians understand baptism by immersion to be a public testimony of faith in Christ and identification with his community of believers. In this context, the symbolism of death and resurrection to new life in Christ is both testimony and visual proclamation of the Gospel. "Christ has given me new life and he can do the same for you!"

Celebration of the Lord's Supper, sometimes referred to as the Eucharist,[51] also is a visual proclamation of the Gospel. When Jesus celebrated the Passover with his disciples on the night before his crucifixion, he infused new meaning into the bread and the wine (Matthew 26:26-28). A festival commemorating Israel's deliverance from Egypt was transformed, that night, into a celebration of the oneness of the church with Christ, its redeemer and Lord.

Just as bread and wine sustain life, so Christ is the source of life for the church (cf. John 15:4-5). Drinking the wine is symbolic of the believer's participation in Christ's death (the wine reminds us of his blood) that cleanses us from all sin (1 John 1:7). In many cultures, including the one in which Jesus lived, bread is "the staff of life." Eating the bread is symbolic of the believer's participation in Christ's body (1 Corinthians 10: 16-17), of the sustaining power of Christ's life in us (John 6:32-35). The Lord's Supper is more, however, than a celebration of Christ's death and our union with him. It also anticipates the day the church will celebrate that supper again in Christ's heavenly Kingdom (Matthew 26:29).

The New Testament writers use various metaphors to help us understand the nature of the church. A powerful metaphor is that of marriage. When teaching believers in Ephesus about God's standards for Christian marriage, Paul draws an analogy between husbands and wives and Christ and the church (Ephesians 5:22-33). A wife should submit to the leadership of her husband as the church submits to Christ. A husband, on the other hand,

---

[51] "Eucharist" comes from the Greek word for "thanksgiving," reflecting the fact that Jesus "gave thanks" when he instituted this celebration, prior to his crucifixion (Matthew 26:27). It typically reflects a view of the Lord's Supper by which grace is received in or with the bread and the wine.

should love his wife with the same self-sacrificing love Christ demonstrated in his life and death for the church.[52] A husband should "nourish and cherish" his wife just as Christ nourishes and cherishes the church. The marriage metaphor is prefigured in Hosea's depiction of idolatrous Israel as an adulterous wife (cf. Hosea 3:1-3) and in Jesus' parable of his return as a bridegroom (Matthew 25:1-12). John, also, employs the marriage metaphor as he anticipates "the marriage supper of the Lamb" (Revelation 19:6-9) and the church as the bride of Christ (Revelation 21:2, 9). The marriage metaphor portrays the loving bond between Christ and the church, his people.

Another metaphor Paul used to describe the church is that of the human body (Romans 12:4-5; 1 Corinthians 12:12-27; Colossians 2:19). It is an apt metaphor since, as Paul notes, our bodies consist of many parts but the whole body suffers when one part is sick or injured. Health requires the proper functioning of every part. In this metaphor, Jesus functions as "the head," the control center for the whole body (Colossians 1:18). The body metaphor emphasizes the interdependence of God's people as well as their dependence upon Christ.

The life of the church is intended to nurture unity and spiritual maturity, with maturity measured against the standard of Christ, himself (Ephesians 4:13-14). This mutual nurturance occurs naturally when every member of the community is functioning properly, ministering to the rest of the community through spiritual gifts which the Holy Spirit assigns in response to needs he recognizes (1 Corinthians 12:7-11). Although the Holy Spirit gifts each believer, believers need to be trained, or "equipped," to contribute to the life of the community as God intends. God has provided gifted leaders—"apostles [i.e., missionaries], prophets [i.e., those who declare God's message], evangelists, and pastor–teachers"—who are responsible for "equipping" Christians to use their spiritual gifts (Ephesians 4:11-12). Thus, the church not only teaches and fellowships and worships and prays, it also is a community in which individual Christians are trained and prepared for service to one another and for effective witness to the non-Christian society in which they live.

---

[52] Note that love is a form of submission, since the best interest of the one loved is placed above one's own interests. Thus, the standard in Christian marriage is mutual, self-sacrificing submission of husband and wife to one another.

This is God's intention for his people. He calls us, collectively as his people, his church, to live daily before him as light in this dark world (cf. Matthew 5:14).

## Let's Talk About It

- How does the description of "church" in this chapter compare with your experience of "church"? In what ways is your church functioning well? How does it need to grow in order better to reflect what God intends? How can you contribute to that kind of growth?

- Of the metaphors for the church found in Scripture—the marriage relationship and the human body—which speaks to you more vividly? What do you want to do to help your church live out more faithfully the truth implied in this metaphor?

# CHAPTER 26

## On Mission

American churches, today, are places of worship, learning, fellowship...and programs! We have programs for kids (Sunday School, children's choirs, Awana, summer camps), for teens (youth programs, youth choirs, service projects), and for adults (Bible study classes, book clubs, recovery support groups, singles groups). And then, there is "missions." Missions is viewed as a program of the church, indeed, in some churches as an important program. Nevertheless, missions is not a program of the church. Missions is the purpose of the church.

God is on mission to restore humanity's broken relationship with himself. As we have seen, God created us for intimacy with himself. He desires to draw us into the relational intimacy that has existed among the persons of the Trinity for all eternity. God loves his human creation and has demonstrated his love by providing a path to reconciliation at great cost to himself (John 3:16; Romans 5:6-8; Ephesians 2:4-7; 1 John 4:9-10). God is grieved by our rebellion against him and the consequent suffering we endure (Ezekiel 18:23, 31-32; John 5:39-40; 2 Peter 3:9). The picture Matthew records of Jesus weeping over Jerusalem (Matthew 23:37) offers insight into the heart of God. God calls the people he created to come to him to find satisfaction and rest (Isaiah 55:1-3; Ezekiel 33:11; Matthew 11:28-30; John 7:37-38).

When God revealed himself to Abraham, his purpose was not to form an exclusive relationship with Abraham. God's intention was to bless the nations through Abraham and his descendants (Genesis 12:1-3). Through the prophet Isaiah, God promised that faithful Jews and, ultimately, the Servant-Messiah would be "a light to the nations" (Isaiah 49:6). His intention for his church, today, is the same (Mt 5:14-16). He taught us to pray that God's Kingdom (i.e., his reign) would come and that his will would be done throughout this earth (Matthew 6:10). His intention is that this Good News of his reign in human hearts and communities "will be proclaimed throughout the whole world as a testimony to all nations" (Matthew 24:14). Christ intends his church to be "a light to the nations."

One way the church is to be that light is through the witness of Christians to God's love and grace. We are his "ambassadors" (2 Corinthians 5:18-20) to our neighbors who are far from him and also to other people and cultures that have not acknowledged him as their Lord. This is the commission he left with us, as his disciples, before he returned to the Father, in heaven (Matthew 28:19-20; Acts 1:8). The 1st Century disciples took the Good News about Jesus to every corner of the Roman world. We know from Scripture that Paul traveled and preached throughout the eastern Mediterranean (Romans 15:18-24) and John served in the Roman province of Asia (cf. Revelation 1:9-11). Other ancient records indicate that Andrew, Peter's brother, went to Scythia (modern Ukraine and southern Russia), Bartholomew to Armenia, in the Caucus Mountains, Thomas established the Christian church in India, and Simon "The Zealot" and Jude carried the Good News to Persia (modern Iran). Paul expressed the dedication demonstrated by all when he wrote, "Woe to me if I do not preach the gospel!" (1 Corinthians 9:16). Indeed, to the Romans, Paul wrote:

> I am under obligation both to Greeks and to barbarians, both to the wise and to the foolish. So I am eager to preach the gospel to you also who are in Rome. For I am not ashamed of the gospel, for it is the power of God for salvation to everyone who believes, to the Jew first and also to the Greek. (Romans 1:14-16)

The disciples of Jesus, today, reflect this same dedication. Indeed, Peter reminds us that we should be prepared, whenever we have the opportunity, to witness to our faith in Christ (1 Peter 3:15).

God also intends the church to be "a light to the nations" through the counter-cultural lifestyle of the Christian community (Matthew 5:14-16). The life of the Christian community should reflect the Hebrew concept of "shalom"—life together as God intends.

Christian relationships should be loving. When a Pharisee, a lawyer, asked Jesus to identify the greatest commandment, Jesus responded by pointing to love of God and neighbor. "On these two commandments," he said, "depend all the Law and the Prophets" (Matthew 22:37-40). At the end of his life, Jesus said the mark of his disciples is their love for one another (John 13:35; cf. Romans 13:8-10).

Christians also should be good stewards of their time, their resources, their relationships, and God's creation. In one verse, Paul provided Christians in Ephesus with the guiding principles of an entire economic theory: "Let the thief no longer steal, but rather let him labor, doing honest work with his own hands, so that he may have something to share with anyone in need" (Ephesians 4:28; cf. 1 Timothy 6:17-19). Manual labor is honorable and unnecessary dependency is inappropriate (2 Thessalonians 3:6-12). The purpose of life is not acquisition, however, but generosity, having "something to share with anyone in need." Sadly, pursuit of wealth can be a trap (1 Timothy 6:9). While many who do not know Christ consider pursuit of wealth the purpose of life, the Christian's lifestyle with respect to possessions and money stands in sharp contrast.

The Christian community is distinguished by compassionate care of family and neighbor. In a "dog eat dog world," Christians are different. Children and grandchildren care for their elderly parents (1 Timothy 5:4); anyone who does not, Paul tells us, "has denied the faith" (1 Timothy 5:8). Compassion toward the poor is expressed in deeds of kindness (James 2:15-16; cf. 1 John 3:17-18). Following Pentecost, when the Jerusalem church was faced with supporting a huge number of converts from all over the Roman Empire, they gave generously with remarkable results, both for the care of these sojourners and for the credibility of the Gospel (Acts 4:32-35). Likewise, when the church in Jerusalem was struck with famine, Paul twice collected contributions from Gentile Christians to ease the crisis (Acts 11:28-30; 1 Corinthians 16:1-3; cf. 2 Corinthians 9:1-5, 11-12). Perhaps the most direct teaching regarding care for the disadvantaged, oppressed, and suffering came from the lips of our Lord when he said, "Truly, I say to you, as you did it to one of the least of these my brothers, you did it to me" (Matthew 25:40; cf. verses 31-46).

Christians are citizens of heaven (Philippians 3:20) but they also are citizens of the communities and nations in which God has placed them. He intends that their citizenship should be redemptive within the fallen societies and structures where they live. Paul summarizes the responsibilities of Christians toward government by writing, "Pay to all what is owed to them: taxes to whom taxes are owed, revenue to whom revenue is owed, respect to whom respect is owed, honor to whom honor is owed" (Romans 13:7; cf. verses 1-6). Indeed, Peter teaches that our citizenship should be a means of testimony (1 Peter 2:13-17).

In all these ways, the life of the Christian community, the church, should contrast with that of the non-Christian world. When the world observes Christians divided, contentious, egocentric, and self-serving, it does not take notice. That's a lifestyle with which the world is all too familiar. On the other hand, when the world observes Christians living together in love, caring for one another, sharing with one another and with the needy among their neighbors, and contributing to the health of their society and their nation, the world takes notice. When they ask, "Why is your lifestyle so different?" Christians have an opportunity to witness to the grace of Christ. We live this way because it is pleasing to God but we also live this way to be "a light to the nations."

God's purpose is to call the nations to himself. This also is the purpose of the church.

> Therefore, if anyone is in Christ, he is a new creation. The old has passed away; behold, the new has come. All this is from God, who through Christ reconciled us to himself and gave us the ministry of reconciliation; that is, in Christ God was reconciling the world to himself, not counting their trespasses against them, and entrusting to us the message of reconciliation. Therefore, we are ambassadors for Christ, God making his appeal through us. We implore you on behalf of Christ, be reconciled to God. (2 Corinthians 5:17-20)

Jesus said he came "to seek and to save the lost" (Luke 19:10). This is God's mission and, by example and command, he has made clear that it should be ours, as well. Whether to the person across the street or to the person of another culture in a distant nation who has no access to the Good News, God calls the church to be ambassadors of reconciliation and redemption. As a community, the church has no other reason for being. Every program of the church should be directed toward equipping Christians to fulfill this mission. Missions is the purpose of the church!

**Let's Talk About It**

- Missions—local and global—is the purpose of the church. To what extent are you satisfied that this is understood, embraced, and actualized in the life of your church? If change is needed, what can you do to contribute to that change?

- Why do we often find it easier to engage in mission in a culture foreign to us than in our own? Which entails more risk—to us and to the Gospel?

# CHAPTER 27

## When Jesus Comes Again

There are few topics that are of greater interest to Christians than the second coming of Jesus. The developing history in the Middle East has served to focus the attention of many on the Bible's prophecies about the end times. Prophecies of declining morality, natural disasters (e.g., earthquakes, drought), wars, and famine seem never to have been more clearly fulfilled than in our generation.

Unfortunately, this great interest in the future has not resulted in greater understanding of Bible prophecy. Rather, it seems confusion about biblical prophecy has multiplied. One author writes a book and tells us the Bible says one thing and another author writes a book which says almost the opposite. One could collect a small library of books on Bible prophecy that are outdated by historic events. Every author seems to have his or her own theories and charts but none of them agree. The result is confusion instead of understanding. God must be grieved.

The Bible was given to teach us those things we need to know in order to live a life pleasing to God now and to prepare us to spend eternity with him in heaven. The Bible's message is clear. God is the creator of all that exists. He created us for relationship with himself. We—individually and collectively—rebelled against him and ruptured the relationship for which we were created. Left to ourselves, our situation is hopeless; there is nothing we can do to repair our relationship with God. God has provided the means of reconciliation by, himself, taking the consequences of our rebellion in the death of Jesus Christ. By receiving reconciliation as a gift, the relationship for which we were created can be restored. God's intention to expand the circle of his eternal relationships will be realized, although some whom he longs to draw into that relationship will persist in refusing his gift, with tragic and eternal consequence. These are the themes we have explored in these chapters.

The Bible was not given to satisfy our curiosity. Two topics about which we tend to be curious are the demonic and the future. These also are topics about which the Bible says little. Yes, demons are real, they actively engage with humans, seeking always to frustrate God's desires and to destroy his creation. We know that they are defeated enemies and that they will be banished to a hell prepared for them at the end of the age. The Bible tells us little, however, about their creation, about their organization and ranks, about interacting with them (e.g., to learn their names), about strategies for dealing with them, "binding" them, or "casting them out." As we have seen, the clearest teaching of the Bible regarding demons is that we are to have nothing to do with them!

Similarly, the Bible tells us little to satisfy our curiosity about the future. We are not given names or dates or charts that detail what will happen and when. In fact, Jesus specifically cautioned us against seeking to know God's plans for the future. He told his disciples, "It is not for you to know times or seasons that the Father has fixed by his own authority" (Acts 1:7). On another occasion, Jesus said, "Concerning that day and hour no one knows, not even the angels of heaven, nor the Son, but the Father only" (Matthew 24:36). Even Jesus, during his life on earth, did not know the details of his return. (That is part of what he gave up in order to face life as we do.) Sadly, Satan uses our curiosity about these topics to distract us from the clear message of the Bible outlined above and from obedience to Christ's command to carry the Good News to all nations.

The clearest information we have about the future is found in the prophecies of Isaiah and Daniel, in Jesus' teaching during the last week of his life, known as The Olivet Discourse (Matthew 24, 25; Luke 21:5-36), in Paul's letters to Christians in Corinth (1 Corinthians 15) and Thessalonica (1 Thessalonians 4:13-5:11), and in the Revelation given to John on Patmos Island.

Of these, the prophecies of Daniel and John belong to a genre known as "apocalyptic literature" that was most common during the last two centuries before Christ. The intertestamental apocalyptic writings appear to be modeled on the revelations given to Daniel in that they include symbolic numbers and images that may seem bizarre and that sometimes (but not always) are interpreted by an angelic messenger. Whereas extra-biblical apocalyptic writing reflects human attempts to interpret or project historic events, Daniel and Revelation are inspired. We need to study them and learn from them but we should do so understanding that they are apocalyptic. We must try to understand the message behind the symbols and avoid interpreting them literally. Our safest course, when seeking to understand God's revelation about the future, is to start elsewhere.

Fortunately, there are some things which are very clearly taught in Scripture; it is those things that should be clear in the mind of every believer. One of the clearest revelations concerning the future is that Jesus is coming again. During the last week of his earthly life, Jesus predicted the destruction of Herod's temple which occurred in 70 A.D. (Matthew 24:1-2). The disciples then asked him directly, "When will these things be, and what will be the sign of your coming and of the close of the age?" (Matthew 24:3). Jesus warned the disciples about deceptive teachers and hasty judgments (Matthew 24:4-8) but he also addressed each of the questions asked. The intervening time, he told them, would be difficult (Matthew 24:9-28) but he will return to gather his people to be with him forever (Matthew 24:29-31).

On the night before his death, Jesus also talked with his disciples about the future. He told them that he would leave them and would prepare a place for them. Then, he said, "If I go and prepare a place for you, I will come again and will take you to myself, that where I am you may be also" (John 14:3). The conditional word that the ESV translates "if" is better translated "since"; neither Jesus' leaving nor his return is in doubt!

Following Jesus' crucifixion and resurrection, as the disciples were with Jesus in Galilee, they asked again about the future. Jesus' response, again, was to caution them against inappropriate curiosity (Acts 1:7). After directing them to wait for empowerment by the Holy Spirit, he ascended into heaven from that Galilean hilltop. As they watched him ascend, two angels appeared to deliver the message they needed to hear. "This Jesus, who was taken up from you into heaven, will come in the same way as you saw him go into heaven" (Acts 1:11).

In his letter to Christians in Thessalonica, Paul underlines the same truth. "The Lord himself will descend from heaven," Paul wrote, "with a cry of command, with the voice of an archangel, and with the sound of the trumpet of God" (1 Thessalonians 4:16; cf. 1 Timothy 6:13-15). As Paul wrote under the inspiration of the Holy Spirit, there was no doubt in his mind; Jesus is coming again!

A second truth clearly revealed regarding the future is that Jesus' return is near. James encourages his readers to be patient with one another since "the coming of the Lord is at hand," indeed, "the Judge is standing at the door" (James 5:8-9). Paul also cites the fact that "the Lord is at hand" as a reason for Christians in Philippi to be trusting, rather than anxious (Philippians 4:5-6). Writing to Christians in Corinth, Paul went as far as to suggest that normal life activities should be set aside because "the appointed time has grown very short...the present form of this world is passing away" (1 Corinthians 7:29-31). The book of Revelation begins by stating this revelation was given by Christ "to show to his servants the things that must soon take place" (Revelation 1:1) and, twenty-two chapters later, the last words of the risen and ascended Christ are, "Surely I am coming soon" (Revelation 22:20).

What does "soon" mean? Clearly, neither John, nor Paul, nor any of the original disciples thought "soon" might mean more than twenty centuries. They expected Jesus to return in their lifetime. Every generation since also has expected Jesus to return in its lifetime but the time of his return has not yet arrived. "Soon" in our time scale is not the same as "soon" in God's.

Peter specifically addresses this question in his second letter. He warns that "scoffers" will call into question Jesus' promises of his soon return, asking, "Where is the promise of his coming? For ever since the fathers fell asleep, all things are continuing as they were from the beginning of creation" (2 Peter 3:4). Peter points out that "with the Lord one day is as a thousand years, and a thousand years as one day" (2 Peter 3:8)—i.e., God's sense of immediacy is different from ours—and concludes that God's delay is occasioned by his concern for those who will experience judgment unless they turn to him (2 Peter 3:9). Nevertheless, the end of the age and the return of Jesus is not in question (2 Peter 3:10).

This leads Peter to the third truth that is clear about the future: We must be ready when Jesus returns. Peter asks, "What sort of people ought you to be in lives of holiness and godliness, waiting for and hastening the coming of the day of God?" (2 Peter 3:11-12). The reality of Jesus' soon return bears immediate consequences for the way we live today. Paul makes the same point in writing to Christians at Thessalonica. "You yourselves are fully aware," Paul wrote, "that the day of the Lord will come like a thief in the night" (i.e., totally unexpectedly; 1 Thessalonians 5:2). Nevertheless, this is not a concern for Christians because "you are all children of light, children of the day" and "since we belong to the day, let us be sober," which Paul identifies with a life of faith, love, and the hope (or expectation) of salvation (1 Thessalonians 5:8).

Jesus repeatedly emphasized our need to be ready as he talked to the disciples regarding the end of the age and his return. Just as people in Noah's day were unprepared when the flood came, so it will be for many when Jesus returns (Matthew 24:37-39). Since we don't know when Jesus will return, he warned, "You also must be ready, for the Son of Man is coming at an hour you do not expect" (Matthew 24:44). Jesus made the same point with a parable about a master who went on a journey, leaving a servant in charge of his home. When the master returned unexpectedly, Jesus points out, how the servant fared was determined by his readiness (Matthew 24:45-51). To underline his point, Jesus told a second parable about wedding attendants, some of whom were ready when the bridegroom arrived and others who were not. Jesus drove home the point of the parable by saying, "Watch therefore, for you know neither the day nor the hour" (Matthew 25:13).

The second coming of Jesus Christ is a "blessed hope" for the Christian (Titus 2:13) for at least two reasons: 1) When Jesus comes we finally will see him face to face, and 2) When he comes for us, we finally will experience the full benefit of salvation for "we shall be like him" (1 John 3:2). As the apostle John contemplated this "hope," he pointed out that everyone who shares this hope "purifies himself as he is pure" (1 John 3:3).

There is much we do not know regarding the end of this age and some things demand discernment and interpretation but there are at least three things that are very clearly taught in Scripture: Jesus is coming again, he is coming soon, and we must be ready to meet him at any time. If we understand these things, we have grasped what is most important.

**Let's Talk About It**

- What is the effect when we pursue our natural curiosities rather than focusing on truth clearly revealed in God's Word? Have you seen this in your own life or in the life of your church? Are there steps you want or need to take to restore biblical balance?

- If you knew Christ would return tomorrow, would you do anything different today? Why, or why not?

# CHAPTER 28

## Judgment Day

Benjamin Franklin, with a twist of humor, observed, "In this world nothing can be said to be certain, except death and taxes." Actually, there are people who avoid paying taxes but no one avoids death. The death rate is 100%. In the Garden of Eden, God told Adam, "in the day that you eat of [the tree in the center of the garden] you shall surely die" (Genesis 2:17). Adam and Eve ate and, just as God said, they died. Sin always leads to death (Romans 6:23). Our first parents did not collapse at that moment and return to dust, but dying began that day and continues to the present. On the other hand, at the moment they disobeyed they did die spiritually; their relationship with God was ruptured by their rebellious choice. Furthermore, the same is true of all of us. As Paul put it, "sin came into the world through one man, and death through sin, and so death spread to all men because all sinned" (Romans 5:12).

The insidious thing about death is that it not only stands at the end of life, it is a sphere in which all of life is lived. Death tyrannizes us. In our humanness, we live in fear of death, it renders life empty and meaningless. Jesus understood this; he said that the person of faith "has passed from death to life"—i.e., from the sphere of death to the sphere of life (John 5:24). It also is the reason he, the Second Person of the divine Trinity, became a human and faced life and death as we do. Jesus did this so, by his death, "he might destroy the one who has the power of death, that is, the devil, and deliver all those who through fear of death were subject to lifelong slavery" (Hebrews 2:14-15).

This is why Jesus was able to console Martha, whose brother had been buried, that the reign of death has been broken; the one with Christ will never die (John 11:25-26). Indeed, a time will come when this physical life will end. Those who already have moved from the sphere of death to the sphere of life, however, don't die; they continue their life in a new intimacy with Christ. It is common to think of death as marking the great transition from this life to the next; for the Christian, it is not. As noted earlier, the great transition occurred when we placed our faith in Christ; death simply is the change from walking with Jesus here to walking with Jesus in eternity. Rather than a fate to be avoided at all cost, death can be welcomed, since being with Christ is "far better" (Philippians 1:23).

Death—the ultimate expression of estrangement and alienation— will be "the last enemy to be destroyed" (1 Corinthians 15:26), but when he walked out of the tomb, Jesus triumphed over death! Contemplating this, Paul breaks into song:

> "Death is swallowed up in victory."
> "O death, where is your victory?
>     O death, where is your sting?"
>     The sting of death is sin, and the power of sin is the law.
> But thanks be to God, who gives us the victory through our
> Lord Jesus Christ. (1 Corinthians 15:54-57)

No one really denies the fact of death. It is more common for people to assume that humans are like the animals; we live, we die, and that's the end. Although it is only in recent generations this view has been widely accepted, it is not new. Paul encountered this view in Corinth. In response, Paul pointed to Jesus. If existence ends at death, Paul argued, then resurrection is impossible (1 Corinthians 15:12-13). The empirical evidence, however, proves the opposite. Jesus did rise from the dead and therefore existence persists beyond death (1 Corinthians 15:20; cf. verses 3-8).

Some Christians, recognizing that the majority of humanity is spiritually lost, that many never have heard the Good News about reconciliation with God through Jesus Christ, and that God is both loving and just, have concluded that God must provide an alternative way for people to encounter and embrace Christ.[53] Biblical Christians who take this view typically confess ignorance

---

[53] This view, known as "wider hope theology," is reflected in C.S. Lewis's Chronicles of Narnia (*The Last Battle*, Glasgow: HarperCollins, 1956) and is embraced by John Stott (in David Edwards and John Stott, *Evangelical Essentials*, Downers Grove: InterVarsity Press, 1988). It also is advocated by Clark Pinnock (*A Wideness in God's Mercy*, Grand Rapids: Zondervan, 1992), Ken Gnanakan (*The Pluralistic Predicament*, Bangalore, India: Theological Book Trust, 1992), and Terrance Tiessen (*Who Can Be Saved?: Reassessing Salvation in Christ and World Religions*, Downers Grove, IL: InterVarsity Press, 2004). For a helpful critique of this position, see Christopher W. Morgan and Robert A. Peterson (eds.), *Faith Comes by Hearing*, Downers Grove: IVP

as to how God may do this, whether in this life through means other than Christian witness, through a divine encounter at the moment of death, or by means that are totally hidden. It is understandable that many find this an attractive possibility.

The most telling consideration regarding this line of reasoning is that there is no Scripture that supports it. None! The evangelistic mandate (Matthew 28:19-20) assumes the urgency of decision in the present life. In a critical passage, Paul argues that salvation is possible only through human witness (Romans 10:8-15). His argument is this: Salvation is impossible apart from saving faith. Saving faith is impossible apart from hearing the Good News about Jesus. Hearing the Good News about Jesus is impossible apart from a human messenger. Therefore, human messengers must be sent; Christian witness is imperative. He concludes by citing Isaiah, "How beautiful are the feet of those who preach the good news!" (Romans 10:15; cf. Isaiah 52:7).

It is not uncommon today to receive reports of genuine seekers, most often in Muslim nations, who receive revelations through dreams or visions that lead to their salvation. Typically, however, the message received directs the seeker to a Christian who shares the Good News, either in person or through electronic media, or to a place where the seeker can obtain a Bible or other Christian literature.

We see this same pattern in Scripture. Luke records that an angel was sent to Cornelius, "a devout man who feared God with all his household, gave alms generously to the people, and prayed continually to God" (Acts 10:2). The angel, however, did not announce the Gospel to Cornelius. Rather, the angel told Cornelius where to find Peter (Acts 10:3-6). Peter, then, shared the Good News, with the result that Cornelius and his entire household came to faith in Christ (Acts 10:34-48).

Similarly, when Christ encountered Paul (then, Saul) on the road to Damascus, he did not call Paul to faith. Instead, Christ told Paul to wait for instructions, which, three days later, were delivered by Ananias (Acts 9:5-6, 17-19). When a foreign government official was reading but not understanding the message of Isaiah, God sent Philip to share the Gospel with him from the passage he was reading (Acts 8:26-38). In all of these cases, God used a human

Academic, 2009. For further consideration of the condition of those without access to the Good News, see Appendix E.

messenger. We have no Biblical account of a person coming to faith in Christ apart from a human witness.

Warnings of judgment for the unrepentant (Matthew 13:41-42; 24:48-51; Hebrews 2:2-3; 2 Peter 3:9-10; Revelation 21:8) and the urgent plea that "now is the day of salvation" (2 Corinthians 6:1-2) also underline the importance of response to God's grace in this life. During the closing days of Jesus' ministry, he was asked if those to be saved will be few (Luke 13:22-30). Jesus responded that God's family will be global, with people included from all points of the compass; the more urgent question is one's own entry into God's kingdom. The difference between those received by God and those rejected is not effort; both strive to enter. Neither is the difference access to grace. Both had access. The difference is timing. Those received by God embraced grace when it was offered, while those rejected assumed too much and waited too long. Indeed, "now is the day of salvation" (2 Corinthians 6:2).

Jesus held out no hope for the one who gains the world but forfeits his soul (Matthew 16:26-27). The writer of Hebrews draws a parallel between the experience of the people of Israel, at Sinai, and us today. They heard God's voice but did not obey and died in the wilderness, without a second chance. Our situation, the writer argues, is more dire. "If they did not escape when they refused him who warned them on earth, much less will we escape if we reject him who warns from heaven" (Hebrews 12:25; cf. verses 18-29). The assumption that God will provide a way for those who die without faith in him is an unfounded hope.

Rather than suggesting that "sincere devotees" of other religions will be accepted by God, the Bible frequently and consistently warns God's people against contact with or practice of other religions. Indeed, it was because of the evil of Canaanite religions that God commanded his people through Moses to purge the land (Deuteronomy 7:1-6, 16). Jeremiah ridiculed Israel for worshiping idols that are as powerless as scarecrows (Jeremiah 10:5). Paul observed that the Athenians had an altar to "an unknown god" but announced that he had come to proclaim the one true God, the creator of heaven and earth, whom they previously had not known (Acts 17:23).

Paul also points out that contact with idols is dangerous; those who offer sacrifices to idols really worship demons (1 Corinthians 10:20). Christians should recognize that all other religions are tactics of

Satan designed to hold people in bondage and to deny God his desire for relationship with the people he created. Sincerity cannot substitute for truth and faith only is as good as its object. The Bible offers no encouragement to assume God will accept the errant faith of those trapped in other religions.

While the Bible offers no hope for those without Christ and although Jesus warned that the gate is wide that leads to destruction "and those who enter by it are many" (Matthew 7:13), this understanding of God's truth is so horrific that humility is appropriate. It is not for us to limit God but every indication in Scripture suggests that he has limited himself, choosing only to use humans to proclaim his message of grace and reconciliation. What is clear in Scripture is that God has entrusted to us this Good News and has made us his ambassadors to those who have not heard (2 Corinthians 5:17-21). We do well to adopt Paul's perspective, "Woe to me if I do not preach the gospel!" (1 Corinthians 9:16).

Significantly, there is something else as unavoidable as death and it's not taxes. The Bible teaches that after death comes judgment (Hebrews 9:27). Because God made us like himself, with the capacity to make choices, it is appropriate that he should hold us accountable for the choices we make. Jesus, in fact, holds the authority to judge every person (John 5:22, 27).

When God judges, we are told, the basis of judgment will be the things done in our lifetime (2 Corinthians 5:10). The question will not be whether a person has been "good enough"; God's standard is perfection (Matthew 5:48). The way we have lived, however, is an appropriate point of examination. Actions are shaped by choices and choices are shaped by one's values and underlying worldview. Those who submit to Jesus as Lord will be judged like everyone else but the question will not be our success in meeting God's standard. We already participate in the perfect holiness of Jesus Christ (Romans 8:2-4). Christians are called to lives of holiness but Jesus has paid the price of our redemption and secured our place in his community (1 Peter 1:14-21). There is no condemnation for those who are in Christ Jesus (Romans 8:1).

People whose worldview is egocentric, however, who do not acknowledge and submit to the sovereignty of a gracious and loving God, reflect that egocentric worldview in the way they live. They may appear to be "good people" but, sadly, the way they have lived will condemn them (cf. Matthew 25:41-46).

John records a vision in which he saw "a great white throne" occupied by Jesus, "and the dead were judged by what was written in the books, according to what they had done" (Revelation 20:11, 12). John reports, "if anyone's name was not found written in the book of life, he was thrown into the lake of fire" (Revelation 20:15).

This is a horrible prospect. As a result, many people, both Christians and non-Christians, find it impossible to believe in hell. They ask, "How could a loving God condemn people to eternal punishment for a single lifetime of sin?" This is a serious question that must be faced. At the outset, however, we need to recognize that God did not prepare hell as a place of punishment for humans; it was prepared "for the Devil and his angels" (Matthew 25:41). It is appropriate, however, that those who align themselves with the Devil will share his fate.

We need to notice two assumptions embedded in the question expressed above. First, the questioner fails to distinguish between "sins" (i.e., wrong things that people do) and "sin" (i.e., our willful attitude of rebellion against God and assertion of our right to live as we please). The fundamental problem is not how many sins we have committed (although, as we've seen, those cannot be overlooked) but our sinful, rebellious nature that defies God and offends his character. Today, God calls us to repent and offers grace to enable us to do so. Nevertheless, if we defiantly continue to sin, rejecting God's grace, "there no longer remains a sacrifice for sins, but a fearful expectation of judgment, and a fury of fire that will consume the adversaries" (Hebrews 10:26-27).

A second assumption is that the problem relates to God's love, that a God who would send people to hell really isn't loving. That, also, is a false assumption. As we have seen, God takes no pleasure in the death of the wicked (Ezekiel 33:11), it's not his will that anyone should perish (2 Peter 3:9). He has provided salvation sufficient for everyone (1 John 2:2). How can his love be called into question if people refuse to accept the salvation he offers? As Paul writes, those "who do not know God and...who do not obey the gospel of our Lord Jesus...will suffer the punishment of eternal destruction, away from the presence of the Lord and from the glory of his might" (2 Thessalonians 1:8-9).

No one likes to think about death, judgment, and hell but the Bible assures us these are realities. Death and judgment are unavoidable, but thankfully hell can be avoided. Reconciliation and acceptance by God are available through Jesus Christ. How sobering these realities. How amazing God's grace. How great is his love for us!

## Let's Talk About It

- Why is it appropriate for God to judge both Christians and non-Christians on the basis of "the deeds done in the body"— i.e., the actions of our lifetime? As you reflect on this, what is your response? What does this make you want to do differently?

- Truly, the thought of millions of people spending eternity in a Christless hell is horrific. Some ask if it is fair to them to condition their salvation on the faithfulness of God's people in sharing the Gospel. How would you respond to that question?

# CHAPTER 29

## Foreverland

It is commonly assumed that people go to heaven when they die. Nevertheless, we need to recall the truth of the old spiritual, "Ev'rybody talkin' 'bout heaven ain't goin' there." It is critically important, therefore, to understand what the Bible clearly teaches about heaven.

Throughout these pages we have observed that God created humans so he could expand the circle of relationships that has existed among the persons of the Trinity from eternity past. There is nothing God desires more than to draw us into an open and intimate relationship with himself. God's desire will not be frustrated. Although, as we have seen, many will refuse his offer of grace and reconciliation, those who will enter his eternal Kingdom are described as "a great multitude that no one could number" (Revelation 7:9). Furthermore, our God must love cultural diversity. All the ethnic and cultural diversity on earth will be represented before his throne—people "from every nation, from all tribes and peoples and languages" (Revelation 7:9).

Interestingly, there is much that God has not told us about heaven. We know that heaven is God's home (cf. Deuteronomy 26:15 and 2 Chronicles 30:27), it is where he lives (Matthew 6:9; 16:17). We also know that heaven will be populated by God's people (Revelation 7:9-10), that God's will is done there (Matthew 6:10), that it is a place of joy (Psalm 16:11) and righteousness (2 Peter 3:13), and that it is free from sorrow, death, and pain (Revelation 21:4).

Paul suggests that the curse that transformed God's perfect world into a place of hardship, disaster, and violence suitable for habitation by fallen humans will be reversed. "The creation itself will be set free from its bondage to corruption and obtain the freedom of the glory of the children of God" (Romans 8:21). Isaiah, also, foresees a day when God's shalom is realized.

> The wolf shall dwell with the lamb,
>> and the leopard shall lie down with the young goat,
>> and the calf and the lion and the fattened calf together;
>> and a little child shall lead them.
> The cow and the bear shall graze;
>> their young shall lie down together;
>> and the lion shall eat straw like the ox.
> The nursing child shall play over the hole of the cobra,
>> and the weaned child shall put his hand on the adder's den.
> They shall not hurt or destroy in all my holy mountain;
>> for the earth shall be full of the knowledge of the Lord as
>> the waters cover the sea. (Isaiah 11:6-9; cf 65:25)

Was life like that in the Garden of Eden, before sin entered this world? Peter, echoing Isaiah, awaits "new heavens and a new earth in which righteousness dwells" (2 Peter 3:13; cf. Isaiah 65:17; 66:22). Maybe life in heaven will be more like the life we know now than most of us realize—minus sin and pain.

Not only this physical world will be changed, we also will be changed. We will exchange these dying bodies for new, eternal bodies, like Christ's glorified body (1 Corinthians 15:50-53; Philippians 3:21). Our new bodies will be able to be seen and felt, like Jesus' body following his resurrection (Luke 24:36-40; John 20:19-20, 26-27). Like his resurrection body, our new bodies will be able to do all the things these bodies can do, minus the limitations we now experience (Luke 24:41-43). John tells us that "when he appears we shall be like him, because we shall see him as he is" (1 John 3:3). We will be like him both in holiness and in our new, eternal bodies.

Those who grieve often are comforted with assurances that they will see their loved one in heaven. When my father-in-law, who clearly was a believer, passed away, my mother-in-law was comforted by Paul's assurance that, when Christ returns, those who have died and those who are alive and remain will be caught up *together* in the air (1 Thessalonians 4:17; emphasis hers). Contrasting with her perspective is that shared by a friend who said of his wife, "When Peggy sees Jesus, there'll be no looking back."

We need not try to decide which is right. Every relationship, ultimately, is between two persons and God certainly desires to know us individually, personally. At the same time, the church, the body of Christ, is a redeemed community. It is in community that the richness of relationship is most fully experienced. In community we realize our identity. In service to others, and thus to the health and welfare of a community, we express and experience the love that characterizes Jesus' disciples.

The other thing we know about heaven is that it will go on forever. Paul wrote to Christians in Thessalonica that Christ will return, at the end of this age, to receive his people "and so we will always be with the Lord" (1 Thessalonians 4:17). Forever is a long time! Yet, what could be greater than to be with the triune God, immersed in the intimacy of that divine relationship, forever? That is the purpose for which we were created. That will be the ultimate fulfillment of our deepest longings and desires.

As Jesus faced the cross, the message he left with his disciples was one of encouragement and hope. He looked beyond the cross, beyond the empty tomb, beyond his ascension to the Father's right hand, and beyond his intercessory ministry for us today. He told the disciples that he was going to prepare a place for them, to which he added, "if I go and prepare a place for you, I will come again and will take you to myself, that where I am you may be also" (John 14:3; cf. Philippians 3:20).

We don't know when that will be but this is our eager anticipation. At the close of the book of Revelation, John records the voice of Jesus, "Surely, I am coming soon." John responds, "Amen. Come, Lord Jesus!" (Revelation 22:20). As we reflect on the wonder of eternity in intimate relationship with God, how can our response not be the same? Come quickly, Lord Jesus!

## Let's Talk About It

- The "city" described in Revelation 21:9-27, with its walls and gates and streets of gold, often is taken to be descriptive of heaven, but John says the city is symbolic of the church, the "bride" of Christ (Revelation 21: 2). Why do you think God has told us so little about the geography of heaven?

- I made the observation that "maybe life in heaven will be more like the life we know now than most of us realize." Would that please or disappoint you? Why?

# CHAPTER 30

## Testing Truth Claims and Making Space

In my "Note from the Author," I encouraged you to test everything you read in this book. That is sound advice, irrespective of the source of information or opinions you encounter. God has given us two tests by which we can discern truth from error. As we have seen, the first is the test of rational consistency with God's prior revelation. Truth claims that conflict with the teaching of the Bible, contextually understood, must be rejected. The second is the test of empirical consistency. Truth claims that contradict realities in the physical world (like miraculous claims that are unfulfilled or unverifiable) also must be rejected. God has given us minds that think rationally and he expects us to use them.

Real heresy exists and it is important to be able to recognize it when we meet it. The heresy of naturalism is encountered daily. The heresy of moral relativism also is pervasive in Western society. God expects us not only to recognize these heresies but to be prepared—gently, lovingly—to expose them (2 Timothy 2:24-26).

To recognize heresy, we must know truth. Jesus said God's word is truth (John 17:17). It is God's word, his inspired Scripture, that makes us wise for salvation. Paul reminded us that the Scriptures are useful for establishing and sharing truth, for exposing ungodly attitudes and behaviors, for correcting misunderstandings, and for guiding us in godly living (2 Timothy 3:16).

The outlines of God's truth are not difficult to discern; they are held, proclaimed, and defended by Biblical Christians everywhere. All Biblical Christians embrace the authority of God's truth revealed in the Bible, the triunity, sovereignty, and justice of God, the deity and humanity of Jesus Christ, the "total depravity" of every human,

God's provision of salvation through the substitutionary death of Jesus, the availability of salvation by grace through faith alone, the security of the believer, God's offer of grace for a life of holiness now, the global redemptive mission of God through his people today, the future return of Christ to establish his Kingdom on earth, the eternal damnation of the lost in hell, and the eternal intimacy of the redeemed with God in his heaven. These are the themes we have discussed in these pages.

Sadly, so much discussion about theology focuses not on these truths which are taught so clearly in Scripture and are embraced so universally by Biblical Christians, but on points which are less clear and therefore are subject to varying interpretations. By arguing over conflicting interpretations, we do Satan's work for him (cf. Titus 3:9-11). It is appropriate for us to form our own understanding of Scripture in areas that are less clear, but we do well to hold and to express our perspectives humbly.

Dallas Willard is reported to have observed, "It's hard to be right and not hurt anyone with it."[54] This is an apt caution for us as students of God's truth. As we grow in our understanding of Bible truths, it is tempting to express ourselves emphatically, authoritatively, dogmatically. It is appropriate for us to be clear, but we also must be patient, compassionate, and loving. If others disagree with us in areas of non-essentials, we should make space for one another. It is enough to agree on what is clear. There is room in God's family for various understandings on areas that are unclear. Deuteronomy 29:29 should be our watchword: "The secret things belong to the Lord our God, but the things that are revealed belong to us and to our children forever, that we may do all the words of this law."

That brings us back to the other point we need always to remember. The Bible was not given to satisfy our curiosities but to teach us those things we need to know to live a life that is pleasing to God now and to prepare us to spend eternity with him in heaven. Furthermore, what we learn in Scripture is not intended to make us smart but to make us holy. Neither God nor Satan cares how much we know if we do not apply it. Jesus' Great Commission was not to teach them to *remember* all that I have commanded you, but to teach them to *obey* (Matthew 28:20). As we grow in our understanding of God's truth, therefore, we ever must ask ourselves how we must respond. God's purpose is that his truth

---

[54] Ruth Haley Barton, *Pursuing God's Will Together*, Downers Grove, IL: IVP Books, 2012, p 24.

obeyed would shape our lives into conformity to the character of Jesus Christ (Ephesians 4:15; cf. verses 11-16).

My prayer for you, as for myself, is that God would help us to be "doers" of his word and not "hearers" (or knowers) only (cf. James 1:22).

## Let's Talk About It

- What are the heresies that you encounter most often? How do you lovingly and effectively expose and confront them? If you find that challenging, whom do you know that may be able to help you?

- Clearly, we are not obligated "make space" for any interpretation of Scripture! How do you discern between heresy and legitimate differences in interpretation? How do you deal with others who understand the Bible differently from what seems clear to you? Do you find it difficult to "make space for others"?

# APPENDICES

# APPENDIX A

## Who are "Biblical Christians"?

The meaning of words changes with time and use. From the time of the European Reformation, Christians who acknowledged the unique authority of the Bible and assumed that its natural meaning was both clear and inspired by God were known as Protestants. When 19th Century liberal theology questioned those assumptions, Christians who maintained them took the name Fundamentalists. In the 1940s and 1950s, when that term became associated with anti-intellectualism and factionalism, those who retained faith in the Bible but rejected these errors identified themselves as Evangelicals.

The term "Evangelical" always has been problematic. It is used in Germany to denote all Protestants, including liberal theologians who deny the truth of the Bible. In 21st Century America, furthermore, theologians who call themselves "Evangelical" have expanded, even distorted, the term in ways that betray its original meaning. The public media and polling organizations also use "Evangelical" to denote a population segment that self-identifies with the term, without attention to the authority of the Bible in faith and life.

Recent decades also have seen a seismic shift in the way texts are interpreted. For centuries it was assumed that authors intended to communicate a message and the task of readers was to discern, by careful attention to the text, the intent of the author. Judgments about the truth or error of the author's intended message were understood to be appropriate and important but the first task of a reader was to understand the author's intent.

The discipline of interpreting texts is called "hermeneutics." Classical hermeneutics focused on the meaning of words, grammatical constructions, the immediate and broader context of statements within a text, and the historical and cultural milieu of the author and the original readers. By the disciplined application of rules of hermeneutics, it was assumed we could recognize and understand the message an author—ancient or contemporary— intended to communicate.

In the 20ᵗʰ Century an alternative hermeneutic challenged these assumptions. Postmodern philosophy questions our capacity to know anything objectively, since all knowledge is seen as constructed from each individual's limited experience. (This development is examined in Chapter 2.) One effect of this philosophy is to discount the possibility—and, therefore, the need—to perceive an author's intent when studying a text, whether contemporary or ancient. Thus, in place of the question "What did this author intend to say?" the focus of postmodern hermeneutics is shifted to "What does this text say to me?"

The personal implications of things we read—the lessons we draw from them—certainly are important, whether or not those lessons were intended by the author. Nevertheless, it is neither honest nor helpful to deny that an author intends to communicate a message or to assume that an author's intended message is unknowable or unimportant. This is especially critical when the text is the Bible, whose ultimate author is God.

To avoid these confusions, I have adopted the term "Biblical Christians" to refer to persons of all Christian traditions—Catholic, Orthodox, Protestant, or Pentecostal/Charismatic—who affirm the unique authority of the Bible for faith and life, who recognize the critical importance of determining the intended meaning of the Biblical text, and who assume that the words of the Bible, understood grammatically, contextually, and culturally, as the authors intended, are inspired by God for our instruction and guidance.

# APPENDIX B

## Jesus, Our Example When Tempted

For we do not have a high priest who is unable to sympathize with our weaknesses, but one who in every respect has been tempted as we are, yet without sin. (Hebrews 4:15)

How is it possible that Jesus was tempted as I am? He was God; I am not God. How is it possible for Jesus to "sympathize with [my] weaknesses" as I face temptations to sin?

These questions have been addressed often by theologians and biblical scholars over the centuries. Historically, discussion has focused on the theoretical question whether it was possible for Jesus to sin[55]—"theoretical," since the Bible clearly teaches that Jesus did not sin (2 Corinthians 5:21; 1 Peter 2:22; 1 John 3:5; cf. John 8:46). Sadly, not only is this discussion speculative, debate often has been decided by appeal to the role of Jesus' human and divine natures. Jesus could not have sinned, it is argued, because the very possibility of sin is contrary to his divine nature. This reflects a fundamental confusion, growing out of failure to understand and distinguish the meaning of "nature" and "person."

As we have seen, "nature" refers to an essential set of attributes, whereas "person" refers to a self that is knowing, feeling, choosing, and relational.[56] A "nature"—a set of attributes—does not make choices, therefore, it cannot sin;[57] only persons have the capacity to

---

[55] This discussion has employed the terms "peccability"—understood to mean Jesus was able to sin—and "impeccability"—understood to mean he was not able to sin—from the Latin *pecco*, meaning "to sin."

[56] See the discussions of "person" in Chapter 4 and the discussion of "nature" in Chapter 15.

[57] The issue is complicated by the fact that the NIV translators used the term "sinful nature" to translate Paul's word "flesh" (*sarx*, σάρξ) in Romans 7:18 and 25. The word

make choices and, therefore, only persons can sin. Since Jesus was one person with two natures (i.e., two sets of attributes, one divine, the other human), focus on his two natures is not helpful with respect to his response (i.e., choice) when faced with temptation to sin. His holiness (an unchangeable attribute of his divine nature and a potential attribute of human nature) would be violated only if he did sin (which he did not), and not by any temptation to sin (which, in fact, he did experience, in his identification with us).

Although the question of Jesus' ability to sin is no more than a distraction from the real issue, it still is important to understand in what ways Jesus experienced temptation "in every respect" as I do. It is helpful, in this regard, to consider the factors that contribute to the temptations you and I experience.

As sons of Adam and daughters of Eve, all of us are attracted toward sin and are inclined to sin. When presented with temptation to sin, we "naturally" choose to yield to the temptation. We are programmed to sin. Children—even babies—do not have to be taught to be egocentric rather than loving, to over-indulge their appetites rather than to restrain them, to test and rebel against authority rather than to submit to it and to respect it. All of us are fallen people. All of us are born with this bias to respond sinfully. Jesus and Paul teach, apart from God's saving grace, that we are "slaves to sin" (John 8:34; Romans 6:16-18). James points out that "each person is tempted when he is lured and enticed by his own desire" (James 1:14).

All children also are born into imperfect families and into communities and cultures that are marred by sin; our exposure to sinful environments is unavoidable. We learn from others to think and act in ways that are contrary to God's character and to our own good. We construct our understanding of our world from those with whom we live and interact. Nevertheless, we choose how we will respond to our environments. John warns his readers that this world system will draw them away from God (1 John 2:15-17). When we expose ourselves unnecessarily to sinful environments, we make it more difficult to resist the temptations before us.

---

"flesh" is used in a variety of ways in the New Testament but Paul often uses it to refer to our predisposition, our propensity, our bias to sin. In that sense, it is "natural" for us to sin because we are sinful people, but that does not mean human "nature" is necessarily sinful. It is not. Our fallen condition is inclined toward sin but sin is not essential to humanness. Adam was fully human prior to his "fall" into sin and Christians will be eternally human, although freed completely from sin, with God in heaven.

Furthermore, all of us bring our own baggage—our prior involvement in sinful thoughts, desires, and actions—to the temptations Satan places before us. The more baggage we bring, the more inclined we are to yield to the temptations we face. Sinful thoughts and actions leave us vulnerable to temptations that lead to other sinful thoughts and actions. That does not mean we are doomed by our own history—God assures us that no temptation is so strong that we cannot resist it (1 Corinthians 10:13)—but it does recognize that prior choices can make the current one easier or more difficult.

Ultimately, Satan, our mortal enemy, is the source of all temptation. It is his purpose to destroy us and to rob God of intimacy with us. Satan is adept at using our fallenness, the sin-saturated environments in which we live, and our individual history of weaknesses and failures to tempt us to evil thoughts, choices, and behaviors.

Jesus was specially tempted by Satan at the beginning of his ministry (Matthew 4:1-11) and again at the conclusion of his ministry (John 14:30). Like us, Jesus was born into a family, a community, and a culture that was marred by sin. Nevertheless, the writer of Hebrews tells us, "Although he was a son, he learned obedience through what he suffered" (Hebrews 5:8), and Luke reports, "the child grew and became strong, filled with wisdom. And the favor of God was upon him" (Luke 2:40). Unlike us, Jesus did not sin and, therefore, he was not drawn toward sin by previous bad choices.

As a result of the sin of our first parents, we share their guilt as members of their race and we participate in their fallenness, the "bias toward sin" noted above. With helpful insight, Buswell points out that Jesus, though fully human, was not a member of Adam's race.[58] For every person living today and for all of our ancestors, our personal existence began at conception. As the Second Person of the Trinity, however, Jesus existed from eternity past; his existence antedates his birth in Bethlehem. Jesus came as "the Second Adam," the head of a new race (1 Corinthians 15:45-49; Romans 5:12-21). Therefore, unlike us, Jesus did not bear the guilt of Adam's sin or share in the fallenness of Adam's race.

The Bible teaches us that Jesus was tempted by Satan as we are. He certainly faced temptations arising from the sinful environments in which he lived, just as we do. If Jesus did not share the fallenness

---

[58] James O. Buswell, Jr., *A Systematic Theology of the Christian Religion*. Vol 2. Grand Rapids: Zondervan Publishing House, 1963. p. 44.

of Adam's race, however, if he did not naturally experience the "bias toward sin" against which you and I struggle, how is it possible that "in every respect [Jesus] has been tempted as we are" (Hebrews 4:15)?

Perhaps the clearest affirmation of Jesus' likeness to us is found in Hebrews 2:14-18. There we read that Jesus became like us "in every respect." Furthermore, the writer insists Jesus' full identity with us was essential both to qualify him as our Savior (verses 14-15) and to enable him "to help those who are being tempted" (verse 18). Is it not possible that in the incarnation, as he emptied himself of the independent use of his divine attributes, that he also chose to take the "bias toward sin" that is borne by every member of the first Adam's race?

A bias toward sin is not sin, it would not defile his purity or entail guilt, but it would enable him to experience the full pull of temptation that you and I know. Indeed, if he experienced our pull toward sin and yet lived a perfect life (as we know he did), his example for us is all the more powerful. As Peter wrote, "Christ also suffered for you, leaving you an example, so that you might follow in his steps" (1 Peter 2:21).

So, if Jesus truly faced life as I do, if he was tempted in every respect as I am, if his life is to be an example for me, how did he manage to live a sinless life?

Careful study of the life of Jesus provides the answer we seek.[59] Jesus' life and ministry was lived in dependence on the Holy Spirit (Luke 4:1, 14; cf. Acts 10:38).[60] Prayer was central throughout his ministry[61] and he urged his disciples to pray for deliverance from temptation (Matthew 26:36-44). Jesus knew the Scriptures and used them to rebuff the temptations of Satan (Matthew 4:3-10). He declared his absolute confidence in the Scriptures (Matthew 5:17-18; John 17:17) and he chided both the theologians of his day (Matthew 22:29) and his own disciples (Luke 24:25) for their ignorance of the truth and power of the Scriptures.

The Holy Spirit, prayer, and the Scriptures are resources available to us in our battle against temptation to sin. You, I, and everyone

---

[59] For a helpful article, see John E. McKinley, "Jesus Christ's Temptation," *Southern Baptist Journal of Theology.* 16.2 (2012): 56-71.
[60] Compare also Isaiah 11:1-2; 42:1; 61:1; Matthew 12:28; Luke 4:18-21.
[61] See the discussion of Jesus' life of prayer in Chapter 12.

who has lived on this earth (other than Jesus) has sinned. John tells us "if we say we have no sin, we deceive ourselves, and the truth is not in us" (1 John 1:8). Nevertheless, Jesus has demonstrated that sin is not unavoidable for us as humans. By the grace of God extended to us through the Holy Spirit, through the power of prayer, and through knowledge of and obedience to the Scriptures, it is possible for us to experience victory over temptation to sin.[62]

In yet another key passage, the writer of Hebrews urges us to "lay aside every weight, and sin which clings so closely, and [to] run with endurance the race that is set before us, looking to Jesus, the founder and perfecter of our faith, who for the joy that was set before him endured the cross, despising the shame, and is seated at the right hand of the throne of God" (Hebrews 12:1-2). The race he ran for us included not only the finish line—the curse of the cross—but also the triumphant example of a sinless life. We may not be required to die a death like his but we are called to live a life of victory over sin and temptation, following his example by embracing, in every situation, the grace God so abundantly offers through the ministry of the Holy Spirit, the Scriptures, and prayer.

Jesus demonstrated that a life free from sin is possible. He died to deliver us from bondage to sin and death (Hebrews 2:14-15). He provides all that is needed to overcome sin and temptation and to live a life characterized by righteousness (1 Peter 2:24). God must be saddened by the readiness of Christians to accept sin and daily confession as normal in the Christian life. Christ was victorious over sin, in his daily life as well as in his death and resurrection, and he intends us to live in victory, as well. Holiness of life is not attained in a single step but God intends us to grow in grace and to progress in righteousness (Ephesians 4:11-16; Colossians 1:9-12; 1 Peter 2:1-3; 2 Peter 3:18).

When Jesus commanded us to "be perfect as your heavenly Father is perfect" (Matthew 5:48) and when Peter quotes God's command through Moses that his people should "be holy, for

---

[62] I have referred to victory over temptation but you may wonder whether the principal challenge is (a) the temptation or (b) the sin to which I am tempted. Temptation does not incur guilt but sin does. Nevertheless, I find it most helpful to focus on the temptation, seeing avoidance of sin as victory over temptation and commission of sin as defeat by temptation. This is because temptation presents me with a decision point: Will I embrace the grace God offers to resist this temptation or will I spurn God's grace, yield to the temptation, and commit the sin to which I am tempted? The critical moment, therefore, is the moment of decision with respect to God's grace in the face of this specific temptation. Sin—or holiness—is the product of that decision.

I am holy" (1 Peter 1:15-16), God was not mocking us! Jesus demonstrated that a life of holiness is possible for us. In every situation, his grace is sufficient (2 Corinthians 12:7-10).

No one (except Jesus) attains sinlessness in this life (1 John 1:8), but that is not because it is impossible. When writing to Christian in Corinth, God led Paul to eliminate all of our excuses for sinful behavior (1 Corinthians 10:13). Never can we say, "My situation is unique," since "No temptation has overtaken you that is not common to man." Never can we say, "God let me down," since "God is faithful." Never can we say, "The temptation was too great for me," since "he will not let you be tempted beyond your ability." Never can we say, "I had no alternative," since "with the temptation he will also provide the way of escape." When we sin, it always is because we choose to, because we have rejected the grace that God offers. We deserve our guilt. When we resist temptation, it always is because of God's amazing grace. He deserves the glory!

Jesus was tempted like us "in every respect…, yet without sin." His grace, extended by the Holy Spirit, in response to prayer, and in obedience to the Scriptures, provides all we need to experience a life of victory.

# APPENDIX C

## Did Jesus Bear the Wrath of the Father?

It is common, today, to hear that Jesus bore the wrath of God against the sins of humanity, accepting the punishment due to us, and thus became our redeemer. This view is graphically expressed by Wayne Grudem. "As Jesus bore the guilt of our sins alone, God the Father, the mighty Creator, the Lord of the universe, poured out on Jesus the fury of his wrath; Jesus became the object of the intense hatred of sin and vengeance against sin that God had patiently stored up since the beginning of the world."[63]

Although this view is common among Biblical Christians and appears to elevate the redemptive work of Christ, it entails several problems. A central concern is the violence this view does to the doctrine of the Trinity. To suggest that one member of the Trinity (the Father) poured out divine wrath on another member of the Trinity (the Son) misrepresents the essential nature of the Trinity. As we have seen, God exists as three persons who share a common existence. From eternity past, these persons have existed in loving fellowship with one another and it is into this relationship that our triune God desires to draw us, his people. To suggest that this holy and loving relationship turned wrathful, even for the hours that Jesus hung on the cross, is contrary to all that God has revealed about himself.

A second problem in this view is that it casts Jesus, the second person of the Trinity, as a third party to God's response to human sin.[64] Indeed, it is not uncommon to hear preachers illustrate the

---

[63] Wayne Grudem. *Bible Doctrine: Essential Teachings of the Christian Faith*. Grand Rapids, MI: Zondervan, 1999. Page 254.

[64] I am indebted to Buswell for effectively making this point. See J. Oliver Buswell, Jr., *A Systematic Theology of the Christian Religion*. Grand Rapids, MI: Zondervan Publishing House, 1963. Vol 2, p 75.

doctrine of the atonement with accounts of innocent persons who stepped forward to pay the fines, or even to accept incarceration or death, on behalf of another person found guilty in a court of law. That is not, however, analogous to Christ's substitutionary death for us. Jesus is not a third party in the drama of redemption. He, as much as the Father and the Spirit, is the offended one. His character is the same as theirs. Human sin is an offense to the holiness of the triune God and appropriately is the object of the wrath of the Son as much as that of the Father or the Spirit. To cast Jesus, the incarnate second person of the Trinity, as a third party in the redemption of God's people is to misrepresent seriously both his character and his role in our redemption.

A third problem is that this view misunderstands the nature of forgiveness, both human and divine.[65] For every offense—whether personal, moral, legal, physiological, or ecological—there are consequences. We live with the consequences of our ecological abuse of God's creation. When we abuse our bodies, we also bear the consequences of our choices. Immorality—moral offense—also bears consequences that often impact others, even becoming generational patterns that destroy lives and relationships far beyond the reach of the original offender.

In the case of personal or legal offenses, however, the consequences of an offense are determined by the offended. In the case of legal offenses, the state is required to impose a penalty as the consequence of the guilty person's violation of the law. For that penalty to be commuted by an empowered official (e.g., a king, president, or governor) in effect grants that society will bear the consequence of the offender's action. Choosing not to impose the appropriate consequence of the offense does not render the offense less real, it simply commits society to absorb the natural and relational pain and disruption that was caused by the offender's action.

When offenses are interpersonal, the situation is similar. We have the option of permitting the offender to live with the consequence of his or her actions, which typically takes the form of damaged or broken relationships, or we can opt to forgive. Forgiveness does not dissipate the consequence of the offense. Rather, it is a choice on the part of the offended to accept the offense, thus himself or herself opting to deal with the injury and hurt inflicted by the

---

[65] Buswell also makes this point, although he does not elaborate it as I have. See Buswell, *A Systematic Theology of the Christian Religion*, Vol 2, p 74.

offensive words or behavior. In the death of Christ on the cross, God accepted and dealt with the consequences of the sins of all humanity (1 John 2:2), opting not to count them against those who accept his offer of forgiveness (Romans 4:5-8) and opening a way to restored fellowship with himself (Romans 4:22-25).

Finally, those who teach that the Father poured out on Jesus his wrath against the sins of humanity often hold that this view is required by Scriptures that teach that Jesus Christ was the "propitiation" for the sins of the world (Romans 3:25; Hebrews 2:17; 1 John 2:2; 4:10). The English word "propitiation" means "to cause to be favorably disposed" and thus, "to pacify or calm negative dispositions." The Greek word translated "propitiation" in the verses cited above is *hilastaerion* ('ιλαστήριον). The meaning of this word has been extensively discussed by biblical scholars but conservative opinion is agreed that "propitiation" is a good translation of its meaning.

The Bible clearly teaches that Jesus is "the propitiation for our sins, and not for ours only but for the sins of the whole world" (1 John 2:2). This does not require, however, that he became the object of divine wrath. Indeed, we have seen that this suggestion does violence to the doctrine of the Trinity, inappropriately makes Jesus a "third party" in the work of redemption, and misunderstands the nature of forgiveness. More specifically, it assumes that the only way for the profound offense of the sins of humanity, and consequently, God's wrath toward sin to be propitiated—both our sin and that of every human—is for that wrath to be vented on the offenders or on a substitute. This is to limit God inappropriately. In human relationships, we recognize that there are alternatives—indeed, preferable alternatives—to venting anger, even when offenses are deep and personal. To suggest that offenses can be forgiven does not diminish the reality of the offense or the appropriateness of anger toward the offensive deed. It is not necessary—indeed, it is unhelpful—however, to direct our anger against the person of the offender.

Buswell's insight regarding forgiveness is helpful here. Sometimes "forgiveness" is equated with overlooking an offense, pretending that no offense was given or that a serious offense is insignificant. That is not true forgiveness, as any personal counselor will be quick to point out. When we overlook an offense, the offense remains and its consequences are protracted. Forgiveness requires accepting the offender, the offense, and its consequences. In the death of Jesus, the triune God accepted into the Trinity the pain of relational brokenness that is the consequence of our sin. Once for all, God in Christ conquered sin and death, healing that brokenness. Jesus' resurrection confirms that relational wholeness within the Trinity is restored and that our offense is forgiven. It is into this wholeness that God now invites us.

In an amazing passage (Romans 3:21-26), Paul tells us that God's forbearance with the sins of humanity ended (i.e., the offense of our sin was dealt with effectively) in the death of Jesus, and that reconciliation with God is a gift of grace to be appropriated by faith. Thus, God shows himself to be both "just"—i.e., the problem of sin has been addressed appropriately and decisively—and "the justifier" of those who place their faith in Jesus.

# APPENDIX D

## Calvinism and Arminianism

Chapter 18 noted that Augustine of Hippo and John Calvin were so committed to magnifying God's omnipotence and sovereignty that they failed to recognize that God is "sovereign over his sovereignty." Because Calvin understood "sovereignty" to imply the total independence of God's will, his concept of God's predestination of the elect and the non-elect stands in apparent conflict with biblical teaching that God is just.

Recognition of God's omniscience as the basis of God's election to save those who would believe only came twenty-five years after Calvin's death. Jacob Arminius was a precocious Dutchman who studied theology in Geneva under Calvin's student, colleague, and successor, Theodore Beza. Upon his return to Amsterdam, Arminius was assigned by the Dutch Church to defend the position of his teachers against a group of laymen and pastors who questioned Calvin's doctrine of predestination. As Arminius studied the Scriptures, he concluded that the questions raised were well founded.

As professor of theology at the University of Leyden, Arminius emphasized the study of the Scriptures rather than scholastic disputes but his views on predestination became known. Following his death, in 1609, his students drafted a "remonstrance," or corrective, which they delivered to the Dutch Church. In summary, the "Five Articles of Remonstrance" are:

1. God elects or reproves on the basis of foreseen faith or belief;
2. Christ died for all humans and for every human, although only believers are saved;

3.  Humans are so depraved that divine grace is necessary for faith or any good deed;
4.  This grace may be resisted;
5.  Whether all who truly are regenerate will certainly persevere in the faith is a point which needs further investigation.[66]

The Dutch Church responded by convening a synod at Dort in 1618. Commitment to Calvin's views was so strong in the Dutch Church that the "Remonstrance" was denounced as heresy (a most unfortunate error, in itself) and the teaching of the church was set forth in five contrasting points known to theological students as TULIP:

T   Total depravity (Affirmation of Point 3 of "The Remonstrance")
U   Unconditional election (Denial of Point 1)
L   Limited atonement (Denial of Point 2)
I   Irresistible grace (Denial of Point 4)
P   Perseverance of the Saints (Denial of Point 5)

Despite all the heat this discussion generates in many quarters, a more sober and biblical view begins by recognizing that there are millions of Biblical Christians in the global church who embrace each perspective. Neither Calvinism nor Arminianism is heresy, although both have generated unbiblical extremes. Some Calvinists and some Arminians also have wandered into heresies that have nothing to do with the understandings of salvation that divide them.

Points on which Calvinists and Arminians are in full agreement far outweigh those on which they disagree. For example, both Biblical Calvinists and Biblical Arminians agree that:

* God eternally exists as Trinity
* The sixty-six books of the Bible are totally trustworthy and are an authoritative standard in all issues of faith and practice
* God has elected (i.e., chosen) all those whom he will save
* Every person apart from Christ is enslaved by sin and hopelessly lost
* Humans are completely unable by their own will or in their own strength to save themselves

---

[66] For the full text, see Phillip Schaff, *The Creeds of Christendom*, Vol 3, pp. 545–549. (Available online at: http://www.ccel.org/ccel/schaff/creeds3.iv.xv.html Accessed August 18, 2016.)

- Jesus Christ, the eternally existing Second Person of the Trinity, became fully human in order to obtain our redemption
- Christ saves those who place their faith in him
- God intends his children to be assured of their salvation

Both Calvinism and Arminianism are consistent systems. The point at which they divide is the basis of God's election of those whom he will save. Calvinists, as we have seen, begin by affirming God's "sovereignty" as unaffected by anything. From this, Calvinists conclude that the basis of God's election of those to be saved was his own will and his will alone. Arminians also affirm God's "sovereignty," but recognize that God is omniscient and just, that he exercises his sovereignty in keeping with his other attributes. From this Arminians conclude that God's election of those to be saved took into consideration God's foreknowledge of each individual's response to God's grace.[67] The "five points of Calvinism" (i.e., TULIP) are logical extensions from the first set of assumptions; the five points of the Remonstrance are logical extensions from the second.

Inasmuch as the two systems disagree, it is reasonable to conclude that one is right and the other wrong—or, perhaps that both are partly right and partly wrong. Rather than trying to disprove one or the other of these positions, however, we will gain more by appreciating the strength of each.

Calvinists are eager to magnify God's glory and to denounce anything that might appear to diminish his glory. Arminians affirm God's glory but also lift up God's justice. They hold that God's decision to create humans in his own image included the capacity for us to make meaningful decisions just as God does, decisions that bear consequences. Arminians also hold God will not violate his image in us by ignoring or overruling choices we make. Calvinists,

---

[67] Some object that conditioning election on foreknown response to grace means that salvation depends on something done by the sinner. This seems to reduce salvation to a matter of "works," which clearly is unbiblical (Ephesians 2:8-9). The flaw in this objection, however, is a misunderstanding of the nature of human choice and the role of God's grace. When God created humans in his image, he gave us the capacity to make real choices. Exercising that capacity is not a work of merit; any merit or guilt pertains to the thing chosen and the resulting actions, rather than to the choice per se. When confronted with God's offer of salvation, the only "work" I can bring is my guilt before a holy God. It's only by God's enabling grace that I am able to choose to embrace the salvation he offers. If I choose to reject that grace, I have no excuse. If I choose to embrace his grace, I deserve no credit; the glory belongs only to Him.

of course, also affirm God's creation of humans in his image and God's justice in his relationships with people, just as Arminians affirm God's absolute sovereignty and seek his glory.

The points on which Calvinists and Arminians disagree are not insignificant but they also are not issues of orthodoxy and heresy. All those who place their faith in Christ, including many, many Calvinists and many, many Arminians, will share heaven. At that point, no doubt, there will be regret for some things said and for ways we have treated one another.

# APPENDIX E

## What About Those Who Have Never Heard?

Is every person on earth really a recipient of God's grace? Many Christians struggle with the thought that people who live in non-Christian cultures and who never have heard the Good News of Jesus' death for them will be condemned to hell. If they had no chance, that is not fair.

It is important for us to approach this question humbly, both because it is so important and because there may be things we do not know regarding God's dealing with those without access to the Bible or to Christian witness. Here, however, are some things we do know: (1) God is perfectly just and loving; (2) God created every human for relationship with himself; (3) God is not willing that any person should spend eternity in hell—that is neither his intention nor desire (2 Peter 3:9); (4) God's "eternal power and divine nature" (i.e., his existence) is clearly revealed in the physical creation (Romans 1:20)—no one can plead ignorance of God's existence; (5) sin bears consequences, often for others as well as for the sinner—this can affect access to the Good News for generations to come (Exodus 20:5; Numbers 14:18); (6) God will not reject those who seek him (Deuteronomy 4:29; Isaiah 55:6-7); (7) God's normal way of reaching those who never have heard is through the witness of Christians—that is why he has commissioned us to make disciples in all the world (Matthew 28:19-20); (8) God can, and sometimes does, use dreams, visions, or angelic messengers to direct seekers to Christians who can share the Good News (Acts 10:1-8).

In seeking to understand God's dealings with those who lack access to the gospel, we must not assume that justice demands that each person receives a clear presentation of the Good News. A clear presentation of the Good News never is the first step toward "turning around." "Turning around" always follows a succession of steps in which God intervenes in our lives in order to bring us to full awareness of our need of his grace and to repentance and faith in the One who became like us and lived and died for us. The earliest steps in this process may be very simple choices to embrace or resist God's voice through one's conscience. The unredeemed conscience can be a means of God's grace (Romans 2:14-16). To those who embrace grace, God extends more grace; to those who persistently resist grace, God can withhold future grace. It appears that grace offered and spurned has resulted in whole cultures being alienated from God's grace. This must break God's heart.

John has given us an enigmatic statement which may suggest that God is at work in the lives of those without access to the Good News, even in ways he has not otherwise revealed. John wrote, "The true light, which gives light to everyone, was coming into the world" (John 1:9). John typically employs the metaphors of light and darkness to represent holiness and sin (cf. 1 John 1:5-7), but Jesus also brings "light" in the sense that he brings understanding of God's truth. Jesus is "the light of the world" (John 9:5), meaning that he reveals God's character and provides reconciliation with God through his death for us. How is it, however, that he "gives light to everyone"? Did John (and the Holy Spirit, who inspired this text) really mean that Jesus encounters every person? If so, how does he do this? We must acknowledge that there are things God has not revealed.

Our natural inclination is to choose what is wrong, but with the help of God's grace, every person is given the capacity to choose what is pleasing to God. It would not be surprising for God to work in special ways to bring the Good News to those who have no normal access to the Good News and who yet seek him. He did that for the Roman Centurion, Cornelius (Acts 10:1-48). Perhaps this is the explanation for reports of primitive tribes that have welcomed Christian missionaries[68] and of the many recent accounts of Muslims who were guided through dreams and visions to Christians or to Christian websites where they learn the Good News.

Here's how I understand this: As we have observed, every person is without excuse before God and, yet, God wants every person to be reconciled with himself. So, he extends grace—spiritual help that enables each person to do what God requires. Because every person's environment, information, and challenges are different, God comes to each person in ways uniquely appropriate to her or

---

[68] See Don Richardson, *Eternity in Their Hearts*. Ventura, CA: Regal Books, 1981.

his situation and context. Each individual's response to God's grace is critical, whether grace is extended through God's testimony to himself in nature, through the quiet voice of conscience, through reading the Bible, or through the witness of a Christian. Each person will be judged on the basis of his or her response to God's grace (cf. Romans 2:12-16). Those who embrace the grace extended to them are led to clearer recognition of God's truth, with new opportunities to respond positively or negatively.

Sadly, the vast majority of those without access to the Good News live with the result of their own responses to grace that has been offered. Some, however—the true seekers after God—respond positively. It is to them that I believe God provides access to the Good News, even if he must direct that person to a Christian, to a biblical radio station, website, or correspondence course, or to a copy of the Bible. Many testimonies exist of persons who have come to faith in Christ in exactly these ways.

Whether those without access to the Good News remain in darkness or are led to the light of the gospel and faith in Christ, however, we do well to remind ourselves of the truths with which we began: God is perfectly just and loving; he takes no pleasure in the death of the wicked but desires that all should come to a living, loving, and intimate relationship with himself.

# APPENDIX F

## Attentive Reading of Scripture

Biblical Christians honor the Scriptures. They seek to know the Bible, to understand its truth, and to obey its teaching. Typically, Biblical Christians approach the Bible in one of three ways. We may read it rapidly, to obtain an overview of its teaching. (I call this "Rapid Reading.") There are multiple plans for reading through the Bible in a year and some achieve that goal annually. We also engage in serious Bible study, analyzing texts and words to discern their meaning in the mind of the human and divine authors. (I call this "Analytical Reading.") Sometimes this includes examining the text in its original language. A third way Biblical Christians study the Bible it to approach it thematically, to select a single theme or topic and examine passages throughout the Scriptures that address that topic. (I call this "Thematic Reading.") This is the method of theological study. Thematic reading is useful in attaining a comprehensive understanding of God's truth on a particular topic or, if pursued systematically, on the major themes of Scripture.

All of these methods nourish our understanding of God's truth, they lead us to marvel at the beauty of God's truth, but they rarely draw us into intimacy with the Father. A fourth approach to Scripture, complementary to and dependent on these others, may be termed "Attentive Reading." Attentive reading approaches the Bible with a focused desire to hear the voice of Christ as he speaks into my life today.

Although Christians throughout history have employed various disciplines to cultivate the spiritual life, I find helpful and commend a seven-step approach adapted from Mulholland[69] and Rice.[70] This is not a discipline to be mastered in a day; our sinful nature will resist it and Satan will oppose it. Furthermore, this is not something to be done quickly; it is best to set aside an hour for the first six steps described here. If you wonder how you will find the time, take a few minutes to reflect, from the perspective of eternity, on the relative importance of the other things that fill your schedule. Or, you may want to consider your urgent need for God's power and grace, and your lack of capacity to accomplish, in your own strength, that which is needed. Be encouraged that this habit, once established, will become a valued and jealously protected part of your day.

Step 1: Quieting – Several years ago a devotional book was published with the title, *Are You Running With Me, Jesus?* The author, aware of the busyness of Christians' lives, wrote brief prayers for those who rush into and out of God's presence. While this may hold a superficial attraction, it also exposes a disturbing reality regarding the low priority too often assigned to meeting with our God and listening to his voice.

Our lives are so full...of busyness, of demands from others, of demands we place on ourselves, of concerns for family and friends, of expectations imposed by our culture and our society, of quest for a better life for our families, of the din of radio and television, and of awareness of our own failures and weaknesses. It is little wonder we so rarely hear the still, small voice of God. Yet, how can I quiet my heart? To make a list of things I will not think about has exactly opposite effect from that desired; we think of those things all the more.

A more fruitful approach is to focus on that which is desired. A quiet time and place, removed from distractions, is most helpful. In a spirit of prayer, come before the living Christ and affirm your desire to meet with him, to experience his presence, and to hear his word to you this day. You may want to make your prayer that of the hymn by E. May Grimes:

> Speak, Lord, in the stillness, while I wait on Thee;
> Hushed my heart to listen in expectancy.

---

[69] M. Robert Mulholland, Jr. *Invitation to a Journey: A Road Map for Spiritual Formation*. Downers Grove, IL: Intervarsity Press. 1993.
[70] Brian K. Rice. *The Exercises Volume One: Conversations*. York, PA: Leadership ConneXtions International, 2012, pp 189-200.

Or, there may be other ways you find helpful to focus your heart and mind on Christ and on his word to you for this day, to focus your attention on meeting with Christ, on listening to and hearing him.[71]

Step 2: Reading – Read a brief passage of Scripture, perhaps a single paragraph or even only three or four verses. Don't skip around in the Scriptures but read systematically, staying in a single book for at least a month before moving to a different genre or a different era in salvation history. The temptation will be to read more than is helpful. Recall that this is "Attentive Reading." We do not want to take the words of Scripture out of context, but this is not the time for analytical study. (If that is needed, do that work at another time.) Focus on the text. Hear it. Digest it.

Step 3: Meditating (or, Reflecting) – As you read and re-read the text, observe prayerfully the phrases or expressions to which your attention is drawn. Rice[72] suggests questions that may help us.

What is this text saying to me?
What is Jesus saying to me?
What do I need to hear in this text?
What does this mean for my life here and now?
Why do these words resonate in me?
How does this apply to me?

Don't try to rush this process and don't become impatient. Recall that our purpose is to meet with Christ, to enter his presence, to hear his voice, to experience intimacy with him. As you meditate on the text and reflect on the questions suggested above, it is natural to turn these questions into prayers for clarity and intimacy.

---

[71] It is common, in guides to spiritual formation, to find recommendation of "centering prayer" or "contemplative prayer" as a way into God's presence. (For a moderate description, see Brian K. Rice, Conversations, pp 203-205.) "Centering prayer" entails focusing the mind on a single word or short phrase—e.g., "Jesus" or "Abba Father"— that is repeated again and again in an attitude of erect posture and slow breathing until one becomes unaware of anything else. This can lead to a trance-like state that some refer to as "ecstasy" (cf. Richard Foster, Prayer: Finding the Heart's True Home, New York: HarperCollins, 1992, p 165). This way, however, has no basis in Scripture; nowhere does Scripture commend numbing one's mind. Indeed, Paul tells the Corinthians, "I will pray with my spirit, but I will pray with my mind also; I will sing praise with my spirit, but I will sing with my mind also" (1 Corinthians 14:15). John instructs us to "test the spirits to see whether they are from God" (1 John 4:1)—a process that fully engages the mind. Similarities between prescriptions for "centering prayer" and use of "mantras" in Eastern and New Age Spirituality should alert us to the potential dangers inherent in this way, or path, to spiritual awareness.
[72] Brian K. Rice, Conversations, p 196.

Step 4: Praying – Turn the truth you have recognized into a prayer. It may be a prayer of confession, a prayer of petition, a prayer of thanksgiving, or a prayer of adoration. This typically is not the time to intercede for others; my focus at this time should be on myself and on my response to the word of Christ to me. There certainly is need for intercession for the cares and demands of the day, for family, for one's community, for national leaders, but that is not the purpose of this hour. Here, the prayer focus is on the word of Christ and on my response to that word, today.

Step 5: Resting (or Communing) – Actively accept the provision of Christ for this day. Know that he loves you, that he forgives you, that his grace is sufficient for you, that he desires to walk with you through this day specifically in the areas regarding which, through this day's reading, he has spoken to you. Take time to rest in this assurance.

Step 6: Journaling – Have at hand a journal or notebook in which you note the passage of the day and the word of Christ to you through it. You will find that you are less prone to distraction and your mind is more focused when you must express your thoughts in writing. Furthermore, thoughts become specific as they pass through the tip of a pen. Include in your journal not only what you have heard but also your response. Don't hesitate to express your love for Christ, your weaknesses in the face of temptation, your dependence on God's grace in all things, your desire for greater intimacy with Christ, your commitment to obey that which you have heard and seen today. Write briefly—rarely more than a page, and often half that—and write for God's eyes alone. If we presume to write for others, our focus easily shifts from one of intimacy to one of performance.

Step 7: Obeying – While not limited to one's "quiet time," commitment to live by the word of truth we have heard is an essential aspect of relationship with Christ. Having heard the voice of Christ, we should carry it with us throughout the day (John 14:15).

It is my prayer that "attentive reading" of God's Word will become a discipline in your life through which you experience true intimacy with the triune God.

Printed in the United States
By Bookmasters